Ray + Pat -
Thanks for your faithful
support of PCA.
Rich Connell

SHARING THE VICTORY

FIFTY YEARS. ONE MISSION.

FIFTY YEARS, ONE MISSION:

The Fellowship of Christian Athletes,
A 50th Anniversary Celebration

Written and edited by FCA
Communications Department, led
by David Smale
Cover Design by Mat Casner
Design and production by Mendy Kling

Published by ROCKHILL BOOKS
an imprint of Kansas City Star Books
1729 Grand Boulevard
Kansas City, Missouri USA 64108

First edition

Library of Congress
Control Number: 2003113116

ISBN: 0974601209

Printed in China
by Terrell Creative

To order copies call StarInfo,
(816) 234-4636. For more information
about this and other fine books from
Kansas City Star Books visit our Web site
at www.thekansascitystore.com.

Acknowledgements

It took 50 years to make the history of FCA to this point, and seems like only slightly less time to assemble all the parts for this book. I want to thank each person who played a role in the production of *Sharing The Victory*, the 50th anniversary of FCA.

The FCA Communications Department (David Smale, Debbie Snow, Jill Ewert and Mat Casner) has worked tirelessly to write, edit, proof and coordinate the production of the book. Many others contributed to the process by giving their time in the proofreading effort. They are greatly appreciated, as well.

Wayne Atcheson, a former FCA staff member, also helped with some of the research and wrote several of the articles from the distant past. He had first-hand knowledge of many of the events, and his clever way of telling the story will enhance your reading pleasure.

The Kansas City Star has been a great partner in the project. From Doug Weaver, who heads the books division at *The Star*, to project manager Doug Worgul, to book designer Mendy Kling, each person in the process has been a great help to FCA.

The many people who are featured in this book also deserve a pat on the back. Many of them retold their stories and/or supplied artifacts that bring the past to life. For every story that's told, there are a thousand others that could have been told. Our goal from the beginning was to tell the history in such a way that any person who ever has been touched by FCA would be able to substitute a name or a date and say, "That could be my story." I pray that we succeeded.

Most of all, I want to thank you. FCA did not get to be the nation's lead-ing sports ministry without the help of thousands of coaches, athletes, administrators, parents, donors, trustees, volunteers and staff. This is your history. I pray that you will enjoy reliving it.

Keep on keepin'on,

Dal Shealy
President/CEO

Table of Contents

(continued)

(continued)

FUTURE

Warmest congratulations to the Fellowship of Christian Athletes on the anniversary of their first fifty years of service for Christ!

Beginning with the vision and dedicated work of only a few individuals, FCA has grown into the most extensive ministry of its type in the world. Through its outreach, it has touched countless thousands of young people and adults for Christ through their shared interest in athletics. Not only that, but through the example and witness of those individuals, FCA has influenced our whole nation for good. In the midst of a changing and complex world, FCA's purpose has not changed: to see the world impacted for Jesus Christ through the influence of athletes and coaches. May it remain ever faithful to that goal.

I thank God for raising up the Fellowship of Christian Athletes and using it so effectively during this past half century. Repeatedly, I have seen its positive impact on people I have met all over the world--including some in my own family.

My prayer is that these past fifty years will be the foundation for an even greater era of faithful service in coming years, as together you "run with endurance the race that is set before us, fixing our eyes on Jesus" (Hebrews 12:1-2, NASB).

Again, my heartfelt congratulations and best wishes to all the FCA family on this happy occasion.

Cordially,

Billy Graham

50 Years, One Mission

It began with a handful of men; it's now impacting the lives of millions of men, women and children every year.

It started as an idea and became a "movement"; it's now the largest ministry of its kind in the world.

It was set in motion on a college campus in Oklahoma; it's now moving on nearly 10,000 junior high, high school and college campuses in the United States.

It was created as a way for athletes and coaches to use the influence they have in society to reach their fellow athletes and coaches, as well as the rest of society, with the Good News of Jesus Christ.

Some things never change.

The Fellowship of Christian Athletes is turning 50, and it still holds to the same mission it's always had: "to present to athletes and coaches and all whom they influence, the challenge and adventure of receiving Jesus Christ as Savior and Lord, serving Him in their relationships and in the fellowship of the church."

† † †

In 1947, Don McClanen, a young Navy veteran, used the GI Bill to enroll at Oklahoma A&M (now Oklahoma State in Stillwater) with an eye toward getting into coaching. He tried out for the football team, but wanted to specialize in kicking, before

the days of kicking specialists. He turned his attention to basketball, where legendary coach Henry Iba proved to be a huge influence.

Iba promised to teach McClanen all he knew about coaching and basketball, and offered him a student-manager's job. At the time, McClanen was collecting clips from newspapers and magazines regarding prominent men in college and professional sports who shared their faith in Jesus Christ. He didn't know why he was storing them in his dresser, but he knew he wanted to keep them. It took seven years for the reason to become clear.

When McClanen finished his degree in 1950, he knew he would be hard to employ. Still a member of the Naval Reserves, he could be called back into service at a moment's notice. Iba got word of McClanen's predicament and helped him get a high school coaching job. The next year, the head coaching position at Eastern Oklahoma State College came open and Iba helped pave the way for McClanen to land that job. It was at EOSC in Wilburton that McClanen's vision for an organization to support Christians in sports really took hold.

He held tightly to the belief that if athletes could be used to sell shaving products, etc., they should be able to use their influence to "sell" the message of Jesus.

On repeated trips back to Stillwater, Okla., McClanen spent considerable time with campus minister Bob Geller, using Geller as a sounding board for his idea.

In March of 1954, McClanen saw that Dr. Louis Evans, one of the men whose story was in his dresser, was to appear in Oklahoma City. Unfortunately in his eyes—his team had a game that night—so McClanen was unable to attend the event.

"As badly as I wanted to hear Dr. Evans, I realized that there was no way I could. I fretted and fumed about it. It seemed so right with all of my thoughts, prayers and dreams." Little did McClanen know that the very next night he would have an opportunity not only to hear Evans speak, but to present his ideas to him.

Prayer remains central to the focus of this athletic ministry.

McClanen and his wife, Gloria, had planned to watch an NCAA regional basketball tournament in Stillwater as the guests of the Gellers. The Gellers had another guest that night—Dr. Evans. After enjoying dinner, McClanen explained his idea to Evans, who thought the idea had to have been shared previously. "Well son, this is wonderful," McClanen remembers Evans saying. "But this is such a wonderful idea that it has to already be in motion. This can't be the first time it's come up."

McClanen explained that it was new and also told the renowned preacher that he had collected clips of prominent athletes and coaches. Evans had the profound suggestion of writing to those 19 men.

Over the next few weeks, Don and Gloria McClanen sent out letters to the 19 men: Red Barber, broadcaster, Brooklyn Dodgers; Dean Cromwell, track coach, University of Southern California; Glenn Cunningham, world-record miler from the University of Kansas; Alvin Dark, shortstop, New York Giants; Carl Erskine, pitcher, Brooklyn Dodgers; Otto Graham, All-Pro quarterback, Cleveland Browns; Tom Harmon, Heisman Trophy winner, University of Michigan; Roe Johnston, All-American end, Naval Academy; Bob Mathias, Olympic gold medallist in the decathlon; Donn Moomaw, All-American linebacker, UCLA; Biggie Munn, head football coach, Michigan State University; Bob Richards, Olympic pole vault gold medallist; Branch Rickey, general manager of the Pittsburgh Pirates; Jack Robinson, All-American basketball player, Baylor University; Louie Sanporenie, Olympic track star; Amos Alonzo Stagg, legendary college football coach; Dan Towler, All-Pro fullback, Los Angeles Rams; Doak Walker, All-American and Heisman-winning halfback, Southern Methodist University; and Bud Wilkinson, head football coach, University of Oklahoma.

"I remember starting the letter by saying, 'You don't know me but I am Don McClanen, the athletic director and head basketball coach at Eastern Oklahoma State College,'" McClanen remembers. "I went on to write that for some time I had had the idea of forming an organization of athletes and coaches in this hero-worshipping nation of ours. My idea was to form an organization that would project them as Christian men before the youth and athletes of our nation."

FCA was a winner early on with personalities like Branch Rickey (far right, center photo) and Ray Hildebrand (with guitar).

"I also said that no one would ever be paid for this, but we would try to raise money to cover expenses. I closed simply by saying, 'If you are interested, let me know.'"

Much to his surprise and delight, 14 of the men responded. The responses were all brief, but most said the same thing: "I'm interested."

McClanen knew he needed to meet some of them. So he borrowed $1,000 from a local bank, putting up his car as collateral. He traveled to the east coast, where he met Graham, Johnston and Erskine. He also met Len LeSourd, managing editor of *Guideposts* magazine, where many of the clippings had originated.

LeSourd offered great encouragement, plus the opportunity to meet Rickey, who was one of the five who had not responded. Somehow, McClanen knew that Rickey was a key, so he tried repeatedly to set up an interview. Rickey's secretary gave him no hope, but finally told McClanen that if he wanted to drive all the way to Pittsburgh with the possibility of a five-minute meeting, he wouldn't stop him.

The McClanens planned another trip, this time to see family in Pennsylvania, in August 1954. While Gloria and their two children bathed the appointment in prayer, McClanen went to the Pirates offices and waited for an opportunity to share his idea with Rickey.

Rickey was known as one of the most powerful men in sports. In 1947, when McClanen was first getting the idea of what ended up being FCA, Rickey was breaking baseball's color barrier by signing Jackie Robinson to a major league contract with the Brooklyn Dodgers. When Rickey got behind something, it carried immediate clout.

So McClanen sat in the waiting room, hoping for his five minutes with Rickey. The five-minute meeting lasted five hours.

"We struck up an immediate rapport," McClanen remembers. "I presented him with my entire story and dream of bringing ballplayers together to influence young people for Christ. Our talk was interspersed with calls about trades and such, and I enjoyed listening to that.

"It was significant that he knew and respected the ministry of Dr. Evans, and I spoke with him about my time with Dr. Evans and his excitement for the idea.

"Finally, he made a statement that I will never forget: 'This thing has the potential of changing the youth scene of America within a decade. It is pregnant with potential. It is just ingenious. It's a new thing, where has it been?'"

What followed was nearly as important as his verbal support. Rickey recognized that the movement would need funding. He came up with the figure of $10,000 and told McClanen how to get ahold of Paul Benedum, an influential businessman in Pittsburgh who eventually did give the $10,000.

As with anything worthwhile, there was some early resistance. None other than Ed Sullivan wrote a column in one of the New York newspapers that criticized the exclusionary practice of an organization focused only on the Christian message. But Rickey quickly calmed McClanen's fears by saying, "Don, I

✠

"This thing has the potential

of changing the youth scene

of America within a decade.

It is pregnant with potential.

It is just ingenious."

—Branch Rickey

✠

would treat that like a fly speck on my nose. Just push it off and go on."

More succinct was Evans, who said, "Don, you take the C (Christian) out of this thing and you take me out of it." Thus the name "Fellowship of Christian Athletes" was chartered in Oklahoma on November 12, 1954.

† † †

The "movement," as it was called early on, grew quickly. The first events were rallies, drawing individual youth teams from around metropolitan areas to hear speakers about whom they had read in the sports pages sharing their faith in Jesus Christ. From there, McClanen and the board got the idea that there should be a national conference to draw college and high school athletes and coaches to one location for a week of "inspiration and perspiration." The first FCA Conference (Camp) was held in Estes Park, Colo., August 18-23, 1956 (see page 62).

A month after that first Camp, Ernie Mehl, the devoutly Christian man who was the sports editor of *The Kansas City Star*, convinced McClanen of the wisdom of moving the FCA headquarters to Kansas City. Mehl had heard of FCA from Dr. Norman Vincent Peale, a prominent minister in New York. He also attended the first Camp.

Kansas City offered a major airport, the home of the national headquarters of the two major collegiate governing bodies—the NCAA and the NAIA—and was central to the United States. So in September 1956, McClanen moved his family and his secretary to Kansas City to set up a new home for the organization.

FCA was still a grass-roots organization, and it needed a mouthpiece. *The Christian Athlete*, a one-page, one-fold newsletter first was published in March

Jackie Robinson (left foreground) called Rickey
"the finest" man in baseball.

1959. It included the rationale for FCA, as well as news from around the country and four weeks of Bible studies for groups of athletes that were forming. They were the predecessors of the Huddle program that exists today. After a week of intense study at Camp, the students requested follow-up materials so they could keep the momentum going and eventually increase it on their campuses.

That year also marked the first time FCA took part in events in coaching association conventions, a staple of today's ministry. In January, "Biggie" Munn spoke at a breakfast in conjunction with the NCAA football coaches' convention. Two months later, H.B. "Bebe" Lee, the director of athletics at Kansas State University, spoke at the first FCA breakfast at the Final Four in Louisville.

The following year—1960—saw the beginning of the expansion of the Camps program. As beautiful as the mountains surrounding Estes Park were, it was obvious that not every athlete who wanted to participate would be able to get to central Colorado. Besides, the attendance had grown from 256 in 1956 to 624 in 1959, with more than 100 athletes turned away.

The Board of Directors selected Lake Geneva, Wisc., as the site of the second Camp. There were 345 in attendance at that Camp, not counting the basketball coach at the University of Wisconsin, John Erickson. John was a church-goer, but his god was basketball.

He received a call from Frank McGuire, legendary coach at North Carolina, asking him if he could provide basketballs and warm-up jerseys to the basketball campers. Not wanting to leave his equipment behind, Erickson decided to stick around for the week. On Thursday evening, he heard one of his favorites, Bob Pettit of the St. Louis Hawks, share about offering his body as a living sacrifice.

"He cried when he spoke to the boys, and that really touched me," Erickson recalls. "When I went home, I told Polly (his wife) how impressed I was with the Conference and that there was something missing in my life. Then and there, I made a personal commitment of my life to Christ."

Two years later, another coach went to his first Camp, and it can be stated very easily that FCA would never be the same. Tom Landry, coach of the fledgling Dallas Cowboys of the NFL, attended a Camp in 1962 in Estes Park.

The efforts of a few men in early 1954 (above) paid dividends in the lives of college athletes like Steve Sloan (opposite with "Bear" Bryant, left, and Dr. Billy Graham).

"I'm not sure that there has been any one coach who has had more influence (on FCA) than Tom Landry," Erickson said in *Impact For Christ*. "We have had many coaches serve but Tom has been willing to give more time and service than any other in America. The great thing about Tom was that his walk always matched his talk."

✝   ✝   ✝

After leading FCA for eight years, McClanen decided to move on, and FCA was in the market for a new Executive Director. Bob Stoddard had been hired in 1960 as FCA's associate director from an immensely successful high school coaching position in suburban New York.

"In all our years of reporting, we have never seen such an outpouring of affection and respect for any man," wrote Tom Hartley of the *Putnam County Courier*. Former players, fellow coaches, cheerleaders and fans gave him a farewell party that included a "This is Your Life" presentation. McClanen felt that if Stoddard could impact a town like he did in Carmel, N.Y., he could do the same for FCA across the country.

When McClanen decided to resign, the Board of Directors saw Stoddard as the clear choice. Stoddard was just 38 and full of energy. He grabbed the position with enthusiasm, traveling around the

"I saw what took place during a short period of time in the life of coaches and athletes, and I thought this was an ideal platform for me. So I became involved in FCA," Landry said in *Impact for Christ*, FCA's 40th anniversary book written by Wayne Atcheson in 1994.

Landry lent his name to FCA with the Tom Landry Associates program for major donors. He spoke countless times at FCA events around the country, even before he retired from coaching in 1989. He even served as the Chairman of the Board of Trustees from 1973-76 while he still was coaching. During the football season, Landry would host the Trustee meetings at the Cowboys' football offices so he could participate and prepare for that Sunday's game.

Campers get a different T-shirt each year,
but the "Ringer-T" was a staple for years.

country spreading the word about FCA. On one such trip, he traveled with Bill Krisher, who has been part of FCA since its beginning. Gary Demarest, a one-time and future staff member who then was pastor of a church in New York, invited the duo to a game of handball.

The next day, Stoddard wasn't feeling well, so LeSourd, the editor of *Guideposts*, suggested that he visit a doctor, who put him in the hospital as a precaution. The following morning, Stoddard suffered a heart attack in the hospital and died.

† † †

During this time, Adult Chapters first made their appearance. The Adult Chapter is to the Huddle what Booster and Alumni Clubs are to their athletic programs. Chapters are made up of coaches, teachers and school administrators, pastors, people from the business community, moms, dads, and others who come together around the common bond of Jesus Christ.

The purpose of an FCA Adult Chapter is "to provide adult fellowship and spiritual growth while implementing FCA's purpose and programs in a defined geographic location."

This purpose can be achieved by:

• Providing FCA Camp scholarship support for area athletes and coaches;

• Providing encouragement to area coaches;

• Supporting local Huddles;

• Providing encouragement to the adult community through outreach;

• Providing resources to Huddles (people, tapes, books, Bible studies);

• Providing ministry programs: rallies, cookouts, retreats, etc.; and

• Providing funding for the local FCA Office.

Another valuable resource who came to FCA in the early 1960s was Ray Hildebrand, a long-time staffer and volunteer. Hildebrand served in the public relations area for the ministry, and blended his unique

sense of humor and musical talent. He wrote the Camp songs for years, and has spoken and/or sang at FCA functions for the past 40 years. He was inducted into the FCA Hall of Champions in 2003.

† † †

Once again, FCA was looking for a leader. James Jeffrey, an energetic Dallas businessman, seemed to be the logical choice. He had been an able volunteer in the Dallas area after a successful college and military athletic career. He had set the school rushing record at Baylor in 1950. When the Korean War broke out, "Jeff" enlisted in the Air Force. He was stationed at Carswell Air Force Base in Fort Worth, where he was a service All-American.

Jeffrey had been associated with FCA from the beginning. At the first Conference, it was Jeffrey who was on the steps of the main lodge welcoming campers. He drove campers to Camp and was busy speaking on behalf of FCA whenever given the chance.

Growth was the residue of Jeffrey's time with FCA. When he began his tenure, there were just four Camps. By the time he stepped down in 1971, there were 17 national Camps. More than 1,500 high school Huddles were in existence when he was finished.

The most amazing stat, and one that speaks to his undying energy, is that Jeffrey had attended all 96 Camps that had been held since 1956 and had spoken at all 83 Camps that had been held while he was Executive Director.

Sometimes, he visited as many as three Camps in one week, entertaining and motivating campers with his words and his juggling.

In 1964, the first FCA Camp at Black Mountain, N.C., was held. The east coast equivalent to Estes Park (for those familiar with FCA), Black Mountain is located in the beautiful Blue Ridge Mountains of western North Carolina. It is home to the well-known Coaches Camp, which began in 1968.

Another highlight of Jeffrey's tenure was the chapel service conducted at the White House in October

1970. Bobby Richardson, a former New York Yankees second baseman, gave the message. It was attended by 20 FCA staff members and members of the Board of Directors (see page 110).

† † †

Jeffrey resigned in February 1972 and was replaced by John Erickson that November. In the interim, the affairs of the office were run by former Kansas basketball coach Dick Harp. "Jeff let me do everything he couldn't do," Harp said of his duties as assistant director. "That gave him the freedom to do what he did best."

It also allowed Harp to run the ministry fluently as the acting CEO. The Dick Harp Library in the World Headquarters in Kansas City is named for the man who was perfectly content to do the behind-the-scenes work so the purpose of the ministry could be advanced.

Erickson was the assistant to the president of the Milwaukee Bucks after running unsuccessfully for the U.S. Senate in 1970. He also had been the general manager of the Bucks and had the claim to fame of drafting Lew Alcindor (later Kareem Abdul-Jabbar) with the first pick of the 1969 NBA Draft. "It's amazing how smart that pick made me," Erickson jokes.

But there was no joking around about the impact Erickson made in his 16-year tenure as Executive Director. Just a few of the initiatives that took place during that period include the launch of the women's and junior high ministries (see page 114), the purchase and expansion of the National Resource Center (later to be named the National Conference Center) (see page 118), the construction of FCA's first building, the establishment of the golf ministry (see page 82) and the creation of *Sharing the VICTORY* magazine, the successor to *The Christian Athlete*.

In 1973, the Board of Directors was merged with the Development Board, forming the Board of Trustees.

The National Conference Center was purchased originally by Don Lash and then sold to FCA through a grant by the Lilly Foundation. Originally a 60-acre facility, the NCC is now a 530-acre facility that serves FCA and other Christian groups throughout the year.

When Title IX—legislation that made it federal law to provide equal athletic opportunity to females as was offered to males in public educational institutions—was passed by the U.S. Congress in 1973, the Board of Trustees determined that a ministry to women should follow quickly.

Campers get a wide variety of activities and traning at FCA Camp.

Also, when the Trustees recognized that the drug problem was spreading to America's junior highs, the decision was made to spread the ministry to junior high campuses.

The FCA offices had been in various locations in downtown Kansas City since moving to town in 1956, but Erickson knew that the ministry needed a home of its own.

"People couldn't identify with us being on the eighth floor of a bank building," he said. "They didn't know who we were."

After some unsuccessful bids to be a part of the Truman Sports Complex, FCA managed to purchase land across Interstate 70 from the complex. The building, which was dedicated in May 1979, comprised 27,000 square feet and was expanded to 59,000 square feet in 2002. It sits on the highest spot in the metro area and over-looks—literally and figuratively—sports in Kansas City.

In 1982, after 23 years of publishing *The Christian Athlete*, FCA made the decision to create *Sharing the VICTORY*. Named after a Camp theme from the late 1970s, *Sharing the VICTORY* remains the primary communications tool for the ministry.

The magazine features stories about athletes and coaches who have accepted Jesus Christ as their Lord and Savior and have let Him affect the way they compete on the athletic field. It is a combination evangelistic/discipleship tool for FCA. It's mission statement is "to communicate the love and power of Jesus Christ in the changed lives of athletes and coaches through the influence of FCA's ministry."

Erickson resigned to become the associate commissioner of the Big Eight Conference in charge of officials in February 1988. He remains close to the ministry, still living in Kansas City. He hosts the John

✠

It's not possible to gauge the impact of the former self-described "small-town coach from South Carolina."

✠

Erickson FCA Golf Classic to support the Kansas City office. He also leads one of the ministry's longest-running Adult Chapters, still meeting every Wednesday morning at a local Presbyterian church.

✝   ✝   ✝

Erickson was replaced as president (the title was changed from executive director during Erickson's tenure) by Gen. Dick Abel, who came to FCA from Colorado Springs. Abel had served as director of legislative and public affairs for the U.S. Olympic Committee. Gen. Abel had a distinguished 30-year career in the Air Force. The highlight of his military career was helping the coordination of the release of the American Prisoners of War from Hanoi, North Vietnam.

"It still is difficult for me to describe that experience," Abel said in *Impact for Christ*. "It was thrilling and a very special time in my military career."

He retired as a Brigadier General and a manager of programs for the Secretary of the Air Force and the Chief of Staff of the Air Force.

"We thought we'd be in Colorado Springs for the rest of our lives," Abel said. "We loved Colorado Springs, and a business opportunity would have kept us there."

But God had different plans. With the resignation of Erickson, FCA turned to Abel, who had become a Christian through FCA, to "rally the troops."

He brought in Don Hilkemeier as vice president of public relations. Abel and Hilkemeier had been roommates during Abel's tour of duty in Vietnam in 1968. He also instituted the C.H.A.D. (Camps, Huddles, Adult Chapters, Development) program.

"Our idea for development was not just fundraising, but a greater emphasis on other programs such as coaches, Leadership Camps, inner-city and women's outreach events," Abel said. "If we called ourselves a national movement, we needed to be just that. So we set a goal to have a Huddle in every junior high, high school and college in America."

The other big initiative during Abel's tenure was the national launch of the *One Way 2 Play–Drug Free!* program. While it began with Abel still in the president's office, it has been the passion of current FCA President/CEO Dal Shealy.

† † †

Shealy came to FCA in 1989 as executive vice president in charge of field staff and ministry programs. He took over the head job when Abel resigned in 1992. Coming during a time of stress for FCA because of sagging finances, Shealy not only helped the ministry survive, he has led the resurgence of the ministry that not only is the oldest sports ministry in the country, but the largest.

It's not possible to gauge the impact of the former self-described "small-town coach from South Carolina," but it's not a stretch to say that FCA would not be around if not for the tough love he showed. Once a sizeable debt was retired, the Board of Trustees voted to adopt a policy of never encumbering debt to produce ministry. This policy makes it a little more difficult to accomplish the goals of the ministry, but is very Biblical in its approach. Ministry that needs to be done will get funded, without the threat of risking the future of the entire ministry.

Growth has been the key word for Shealy's tenure. Camp attendance now regularly exceeds 15,000 and there are now close to 8,000 Huddles. Shealy has been part of the launch of the chaplaincy program that has placed chaplains on college campuses, as well as on professional sports staffs.

Under Shealy's leadership, FCA has formed and enhanced partnerships with other specialized ministry movements, including the Billy Graham Crusade, Youth For Christ, Campus Crusade, Promise Keepers, DC/LA 2000 and Athletes in Action. He regularly attends conferences with other ministry leaders and was close friends with the late Dr. Bill Bright, the founder of Campus Crusade.

Shealy's vision to see the influence of athletes and coaches reach people for Christ helped lead to the global initiative for FCA. Through this program, FCA established contact with sports ministry leaders in 80 countries. FCA has participated actively in partnerships in Singapore, Honduras, South Africa and several other countries restricted to the Gospel.

In the United States alone, FCA impacts more than 300,000 students per year. Counting volunteers, donors, students, coaches, staff and attendees at FCA events, more than 1.5 million people are reached each year.

Today, people can sign up to be part of TEAM FCA by signing the "Competitors' Creed" (see opposite page).

"TEAM FCA is a part of Team Jesus Christ," Shealy says. If you take Christ out of the middle of the Fellowship of Christian Athletes, you'll have

The message of The Competitor's Creed rings true for competitors of all ages.

The Competitor's Creed

I am a Christian first and last.
I am created in the likeness of God Almighty to bring Him glory.
I am a member of Team Jesus Christ.
I wear the colors of the cross.

I am a Competitor now and forever.
I am made to strive, to strain, to stretch and to succeed in the arena of competition.
I am a Christian Competitor and as such, I face my challenger with the face of Christ.

I do not trust in myself.
I do not boast in my abilities or believe in my own strength.
I rely solely on the power of God.
I compete for the pleasure of my Heavenly Father, the honor of Christ and
the reputation of the Holy Spirit.

My attitude on and off the field is above reproach - my conduct beyond criticism.
Whether I am preparing, practicing or playing;
I submit to God's authority and those He has put over me.
I respect my coaches, officials, teammates and competitors out of respect for the Lord.

My body is the temple of Jesus Christ.
I protect it from within and without.
Nothing enters my body that does not honor the Living God.
My sweat is an offering to my Master. My soreness is a sacrifice to my Savior.

I give my all - all of the time.
I do not give up. I do not give in. I do not give out.
I am the Lord's warrior - a competitor by conviction and a disciple of determination.
I am confident beyond reason because my confidence lies in Christ.
The results of my efforts must result in His glory.

Let the competition begin.
Let the glory be God's.

COMPETITORS for CHRIST

Fellowship of 'ian' Athletes. Ian, in this case, can stand for 'I am nothing.' We don't want to be nothing. That's why FCA is Christ-centered. In all we do, we want to present Christ, crucified and resurrected, inviting athletes and coaches and 'all whom they influence' to receive Jesus as Savior and Lord."

The advent of technology has not escaped Shealy's notice either. In 1995, FCA registered the domain name of www.fca.org. It currently owns nine domain names nationally and more than 50 on a regional basis. In those national domain names there are numerous sub-domains, dealing with every aspect of the ministry.

In the past five years, Shealy has spearheaded the review and affirmation of the ministry's Mission Statement. FCA's Mission Statement is "to present to athletes and coaches and all whom they influence

the challenge and adventure of receiving Jesus Christ as Savior and Lord, serving Him in their relationships and in the fellowship of the church." Following are some descriptions and definitions of each of the phrases in the statement.

• "to present"—FCA is a "presenting" ministry, introducing people to Christ and a relationship with Him. By making a life with Christ an attractive and appealing lifestyle, believers can help non-believers seek answers to spiritual questions. FCA acknowledges that the family and the church are the primary institutions for Christian growth and discipleship, and therefore urges athletes and coaches to become involved in the life of their churches.

• "to athletes and coaches"—FCA is an athletic ministry, its primary constituency being athletes and

"Athletes and coaches and all whom they influence"
come in many shapes and sizes.

coaches from the junior high through collegiate levels. Because athletes and coaches, by definition, have a competitive nature, it is very easy for them to develop an "I did it on my own" attitude, which is the opposite of a dependency on God. FCA uses a language and medium familiar to these two groups to reach them with the saving knowledge of Christ.

- "and all whom they influence"—FCA is an influencing ministry, using athletics as its platform and athletes and coaches as its role models and spokespersons. In our society, athletes are placed on a pedestal and are seen as "experts" in all areas, not just athletics. The general public listens to what the athlete (and coach) has to say. FCA has used this "stature" to reach those who are unwilling to listen to other overtures about a person's faith.

- "the challenge"—FCA strives to present the complete Gospel, in which athletes and coaches are encouraged to "count the cost" and make thoughtful decisions for Christ. FCA recognizes that a life of following Christ is not going to be easy. Simply accepting Christ as Savior is not enough; believers are commanded in the Bible to live a life fully devoted to following Him.

- "and adventure of receiving Jesus Christ as Savior and Lord"—FCA presents the acceptance of Christ as a continuing journey in which athletes and coaches grow in knowledge of and service to Christ. FCA believes that even though the journey is not going to be easy, it is a journey that is well worth taking. Following Christ's footsteps every step of the way can be extremely rewarding in life, as well as in death.

- "serving Him in their relationships and in the fellowship of the church"—FCA aids athletes and coaches in maintaining or restoring relationships, and directing athletes and coaches toward the family and the church. The church is the body of Christ, without which the individual "parts" cannot function to their fullest extent. The life of a follower of Christ is a life of service. The FCA student-athlete recognizes that he or she is only a reflection of God's strength and His grace for salvation. True service means laying one's life down for others, whether that is a physical sacrifice or a symbolic one.

At the same time as the review of the Mission Statement, FCA underwent a pruning and restructuring that was designed to make the strategic plan of the ministry effective. Placing more emphasis on the efforts of the local staff, the strategic plan makes FCA a "bottom up" ministry, with the focus on the "trenches," where the majority of the ministry is done.

Also in 1999, FCA began giving the Tom Landry Excellence of Character Award. The first five years' recipients were Coach Jim Myers, Dr. Billy Graham, Coach Grant Teaff, Dr. Howard Hendricks, and Dr. and Mrs. James Dodson.

✝   ✝   ✝

The FCA Vision—"To see the world impacted for Jesus Christ through the influence of athletes and coaches"—was created in 1999. The Core Values of Integrity, Serving, Teamwork and Excellence were added at the same time. Prayer is at the center of the Core Values and the center of all that FCA does.

Some other highlights of Shealy's presidency include a visit by Vice Presidential candidate Dick Cheney. Cheney came to the FCA National Office in August 2000 to endorse the One Way 2 Play! program.

"FCA is not interested in making a statement," Cheney said. "FCA is interested in making a difference. That's exactly what FCA has been doing since 1954. FCA is changing lives and challenging young people all across America."

The World Headquarters building expansion was completed in 2002.

INTEGRITY

We will demonstrate Christ-like wholeness, privately and publicly. (Proverbs 11:3)

...living and ministering out of the overflow of our growing relationship with Christ.

...being submissive to the Lord and those we serve and lead.

...being above reproach in all our financial dealings and statistical reporting.

...being transparent, honest and trustworthy.

...engaging in accountable relationships.

...placing greater importance on authenticity than image.

...caring more about the lost than ourselves.

...modeling a life with prayer as the foundation.

SERVING

We will model Jesus' example of serving. (John 13:12-15)

...seeking out the needs of others and responding appropriately to meet them.

...seeing others as more important than ourselves.

...spending time with people we serve developing trusting relationships.

...caring about the individuals we serve, not just what they can do for FCA.

...praying for those we serve, and those with whom we co-labor.

...focusing our efforts on supporting and adding value to those on the frontline sharing Jesus Christ.

...giving of ourselves to the work which God has called us to do in our local church.

TEAMWORK

We will express our unity in Christ in all our relationships. (Philippians 2:1-5)

...realizing our dependence on God in the work of the Kingdom.

...reflecting the Body of Christ through gender, ethnic, sport and denominational diversity.

...equipping, encouraging and empowering one another for ministry.

...identifying, utilizing and appreciating each individual's giftedness.

...understanding and respecting the role of each individual.

...having an environment of open, honest and healthy communication.

...celebrating and hurting together.

...working effectively and cooperatively with other ministries.

EXCELLENCE

We will honor and glorify God in all we do. (Colossians 3:23-24)

...honoring our commitments.

...pursuing innovation and creativity.

...valuing quality over quantity.

...being wise stewards of the spiritual, material and relational resources He has entrusted to us.

...being focused on the FCA mission.

...developing effective ministry.

The National Headquarters now comprises 59,000 square feet, including a state-of-the-art training room. No longer does FCA have to rent a local hotel to do staff training or to hold staff functions. FCA also has blessed the community by allowing the use of the facility for training or social functions.

The renovation also included the Tom Landry Worship Center, an envigorated Hall of Champions and the Dick Harp Library.

† † †

In the fall of 2002, FCA crystallized the ministry into the "Four C's": Coaches, Campus, Camps and Community.

COACHES MINISTRY

At the heart of FCA are coaches. FCA's role is to minister to them by encouraging and equipping them to know and serve Christ. FCA ministers to coaches through Bible studies, staff contacts, prayer support, discipleship and mentoring, *Behind the Bench* (a program for coaches' wives), resources, outreach events, national and local conventions, and conferences and retreats.

CAMPUS MINISTRY

The Campus Ministry is initiated and led by student-athletes and coaches on junior high, high school and college campuses. The programs of the Campus Ministry include Huddles, team Bible studies, chapel programs, TEAM FCA membership, *One Way 2 Play — Drug Free!* and special events.

CAMPS MINISTRY

Camps are a time of "inspiration and perspiration" for athletes and coaches to reach their potential by offering comprehensive athletic, spiritual and leadership training. The types of Camps are Athletic Camp, Leadership Camp, Coaches Camp and Power Camp.

COMMUNITY MINISTRY

The non-school-based FCA ministries reach the community through partnerships with the local churches, businesses, parents and volunteers. These ministries not only reach out to the community, but also allow the community to invest in athletes and coaches. Community Ministries include: stewardship ministries, adult ministries, sport-specific ministries, membership, urban initiatives, clinics, product and resource development, and professional athlete ministries.

With the success of the golf and lacrosse ministries, FCA has recognized the value of sport-specific ministry. In the summer of 2003, baseball was added to the mix.

"The advantage of sport-specific ministry is that the ones doing the ministry and the ones being ministered to are speaking the language, even more than with just the general approach of sports," Shealy said. "We are excited about the impact FCA can have in the coming years."

† † †

Shealy is one of the presidents who helped form a partnership between the leaders of the nation's largest specialized ministry movements. The leaders of FCA, Campus Crusade for Christ, Navigators, Youth For Christ, Young Life and Intervarsity meet and communicate regularly regarding issues that cross ministry lines.

† † †

The Mission hasn't changed in 50 years. The Vision was incorporated to summarize the Mission Statement, and the Core Values have been added to show how ministry is done. But millions of touched lives later, FCA still exists "To present to athletes and coaches and all whom they influence, the challenge and adventure of receiving Jesus Christ as Savior and Lord, serving Him in their relationships and in the fellowship of the church."

Fifty years are in the books. As God continues to bless the ministry, no doubt there are many more years to come.

The groundbreaking of the World Headquarters building meant many more years of ministry for Dick Harp and his colleagues.

"Therefore go and make disciples
of all nations, baptizing them in
the name of the Father and of the
Son and of the Holy Spirit."

—Matthew 28:19

Present

Gathering With a Few (Thousand) Friends

Citywide Rallies in 1957-61 and Weekends of Champions in 1967-71 across the United States were powerful events that dramatically propelled the FCA movement.

Professional and college athletes and coaches gathered without compensation to share their faith and testimonies. The nation never had seen such rallies where household names from the world of sports drew thousands of people in the name of Jesus Christ.

The first FCA Citywide Rally was held in 1957 at the Ryman Auditorium, home of the Grand Ole Opry in Nashville, Tenn.

The country music stage was filled with an amazing lineup of athletic personalities of that era. They included Alvin Dark, George Kell, Dave "Boo" Ferris, Don Gutteridge, Adrian Burk, Don McClanen, Dick Harp, Ron Morris, Donn Moomaw, Gary Demarest, LeRoy King, George Selleck, David Switzer and George Vokert.

Nashville Banner Sports Editor Fred Russell wrote, "A powerful force for good is on the move in this country through sports. What has happened in Nashville may provide the impetus for spreading the influence of the Fellowship of Christian Athletes to every city and town in America. These men are pioneers of sort, in the most worthwhile of all endeavors. The wholesome effect that the FCA movement may have within the next few years staggers the imagination."

Russell was right on target. Only three years old, FCA was indeed a movement ordained by God. Through 1961, Citywide Rallies turned into two- and three-day ministry opportunities across the nation. Athletes and coaches conducted sports jamborees giving instruction in their sport and sharing their faith from the platform the next day.⇨

Weekends of Champions and Citywide Rallies brought some of the country's brightest stars to the stage to share their testimonies.

Ron Morris chaired a Dallas Citywide Rally in January 1959. Twenty-five athletes and coaches participated. Tulsa followed in February with Carl Erskine, Donn Moomaw, Pepper Martin, Don Meredith and George Kell. Springfield, Mass. held a Citywide Rally that featured Otto Graham. It was the first FCA opportunity in New England, with Dick Armstrong of the Baltimore Orioles coordinating.

Other towns and cities that followed included Jacksonville, Fla.; Wilmington, Del.; Columbia, S.C.; Seattle; Lubbock, Texas; and Bristol, Tenn. Lives were changed by the powerful influences of Christian athletes and coaches. At the same time, FCA was gaining attention and was being embraced warmly by people across America.

From 1967-71, Weekends of Champions were overwhelmingly successful for FCA. Kansas City became the first Weekend of Champions site in February 1967. Professional and college athletes and coaches converged on the city. The format included school assemblies on Friday, appearances in juvenile centers and sports clinics on Saturday, a banquet on Saturday evening, messages in churches on Sunday morning and a rally on Sunday afternoon. A crowd of 11,000 people gathered in Municipal Auditorium in one memorable FCA occasion.

That same weekend schedule was repeated for the next four years. In 1968, Wichita, Kan., had 12,000 people for its rally. In Albuquerque, N.M., the event reached 200,000 people, an incredible outreach for such a young movement.

In 1969, 161 college and pro athletes covered the city of Dallas. It was one of the largest groups of well-known athletes ever assembled to minister in one area. The rally speakers included Bart Starr, Jerry Stovall, Paul Anderson and Tom Landry.

✠

"The wholesome effect that the FCA movement may have within the next few years staggers the imagination."

✠

—*Nashville Banner* Sports Editor Fred Russell

But no Weekend of Champions could rival the setting of the 1971 gathering in Miami on Super Bowl V weekend. After sharing the Gospel for three days, the 100 athletes and coaches met at the Orange Bowl that Sunday afternoon for the game. The Super Bowl participants, the Dallas Cowboys and Baltimore Colts, provided the tickets at no charge.

FCA now has Huddles in 47 states, reaching approximately 350,000 students. While the students being ministered to today through FCA were not born during this era, the momentum FCA gained through Citywide Rallies and Weekends of Champions played an integral role in the early growth of this successful ministry. ✟

America seemed ready for the FCA ministry.

True Strength

What do you call a man who lifts two 85-pound dumbbells with his little fingers, hammers a twenty-penny nail through a two-inch board with his fist or hoists eight football players weighing more than 2,000 pounds combined? A modern-day Samson? A wonder of nature? The world's strongest man? How about "nothing without the strength of Christ"?

That's how Paul Anderson described himself. "I am the world's strongest man, but I can't get through one day without the strength of Jesus Christ," he would tell a room full of engrossed young men.

"Those who felt that Christianity was for sissies changed their minds after hearing Paul," wrote Wayne Atcheson in his 1994 book, *Impact For Christ*. "He made an unforgettable impression and impact."

Anderson won the Olympic gold medal in weightlifting in the super heavyweight division at the 1956 Games in Melbourne, Australia. Facing a 104-degree fever that seriously jeopardized his chances, he called on the strength of God on his last attempt and subsequently lifted the bar over his head.

In 1957, in his hometown of Toccoa, Ga., Anderson squatted under a table that, with the contents on

the table, weighed 6,270 pounds—the equivalent of more than 31 average-sized adult men—and lifted it off the ground. The *Guiness Book of World Records* recognized it as the "greatest weight ever raised by a human being," bettering the old record by more than 2,000 pounds.

Anderson was not a tall man, though at 5-9 and 375 pounds, he probably wasn't picked on too often on the street corner. Throughout the 1960s and '70s, he traveled throughout the country showing feats of strength and then sharing the Source of his true strength.

"Paul was a willing servant," Atcheson wrote. "FCA audiences in the four corners of the United States have sat before his amazing feats of strength and have heard his clear presentation of the Gospel. He was a force like none other for the Lord."

Kidney diseases took his physical strength in the early 1980s, and eventually took his life in 1994. By then he could trade all the other monikers for the one he most wanted to hear.

No doubt, as he took his first step into Heaven, he heard, "Well done, good and faithful servant."✞

The "world's strongest man" drew all his strength
from the Lord.

A Variety of Purposes;
a Multitude of Results

"Inspiration and perspiration." Few phrases more accurately describe what happens in a young person's life at FCA Camp. Camp Week begins with an assembly hall full of strangers and ends with a community of inseparable friends.

A key ingredient to the relationships developed at Camp are the Huddles, the small groups of campers and their Huddle Leaders. The secret to the success is in the careful formation of each Huddle. Campers are not placed with their friends from home, which instantly levels the playing field between those who have many friends and those who do not.

When young athletes are given the opportunity to spend a week with new friends, they get a chance

to view life from a new angle. At the beginning of the week, campers barely speak to one another. But by the end of the week, after sweating, talking, praying and worshipping together, they are seen exchanging e-mail addresses and phone numbers with their new friends.

It would be easy to think that the most influential people at Camp are the speakers or coaches. While they do have a wonderful and tremendous impact, the most influential people are the Huddle Leaders— typically college athletes who love Jesus and want to help campers come to know and to love Him.

Huddle Leaders are with the campers 24 hours a day. They sleep in the same dorm. They eat together. ⇨

FCA Camp always has been a week of "inspiration...

They work out together. They compete together. They study the Bible together. Huddle Leaders are skillfully trained and have the amazing power of the Holy Spirit to guide them. They certainly leave a permanent imprint on each camper's life.

For five days, campers are surrounded by a completely positive environment. They come from every state, from every racial background, from every type of family and from many spiritual maturity levels. For five days they receive love and encouragement without the negative things that can pull them down in everyday life. Campers leave on a "high," wishing that they could stay in that environment forever.

The four different Camps (Athletic, Leadership, Coaches and Power Camps) have given FCA the opportunity to impact different populations. Those attending Athletic Camps are given instruction on specific sports, while focusing on Christ. Leadership Camps offer campers practical disciplines for a deeper walk with Christ, and they are taught how to minister effectively on campus. Coaches can attend a

week of FCA Coaches Camp for a chance to be encouraged and to learn from like-minded individuals with the same profession. Power Camps focus on kids under the age of 13—the population with the greatest probability of accepting Christ as their Savior.

Every summer at the conclusion of the Camp season, FCA staff members are blessed with the reports of lives changed eternally through the Camp ministry. Whether they are inner-city kids who never before had heard Jesus' name outside of profanity, college coaches who used to believe that the scoreboard was the only way to measure success, or future leaders of our country who are beginning to understand what godly leadership is all about, nothing impacts a person like a week at FCA Camp.

Legendary basketball coach John Wooden once said, "You'll be no saint after leaving an FCA Conference, but you'll be a better person than you were."✝

...and perspiration."

"*They eat together.*

They work out together.

They compete together.

They study the Bible together."

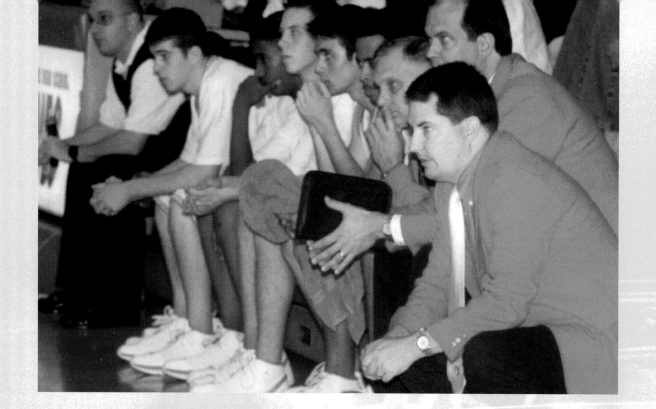

'The Coolest Part of Camp'

In the summer of 2001, Coach Mark Rickman loaded up 10 members of his Boone High School (Fla.) boys basketball team and headed to a North Carolina FCA Camp. Of the 10, none had solid relationships with Christ when the week began. By week's end, however, all would acknowledge Jesus as their personal Savior—seven new commitments, three rededications and one incredible team.

That team, composed of the 10 new Christians and two believers who were not able to attend the Camp, had no player taller than 6-foot-3, yet still clawed their way to the 2002 Class 6A state finals. They led two-time defending champion Fort Lauderdale Dillard with just under 3 minutes remaining, but fell just short of the title, losing 52-48.

"As painful as losing the state championship was, I wouldn't trade what happened up in North Carolina for any championship trophy or gold medal," Rickman said. "I don't think you could go anywhere in the nation, on any team, girls or boys, and find a whole team of Christians."

The team unity that was formed in North Carolina was acknowledged in the local papers, leading *Orlando Sentinel* columnist Mike Bianchi to address the issue after Boone's state championship loss:

"Maybe there is something to this corny camaraderie stuff. Maybe that's the only way you can explain the Boone Braves playing for the state championship when they really had no business being on the same floor as Dillard."

The on-court change in the Boone players also was noticed by their opponents. At a February FCA-sponsored Night of Champions, Boone senior Josh Shave, a featured speaker for the event, shared the following story:

"A rival player walked up to me after a game and said, 'You know, I was watching you (during the game), and I could tell you were different out there. I could see the difference. Now I know why.'"

Shave and his teammates credit this incredible change to their coach and the FCA Camp experience.

"I think it is awesome how the whole Camp is based on Christ," Shave said. "I love to play sports, but I think it's awesome that it is all for God's glory. When you're at Camp, you're there to glorify God, but you're still playing a sport you love so much.

"We really looked forward to playing basketball, but we looked forward to learning about God even more as the week went on. To be able to play the sport I love and do it all for God was the coolest part of Camp."✝

The unity of the Boone High School basketball team began at FCA Camp.

Chalk Talk

"Brawny coaches stare incredulously. Athletes suspect a put-on. An artist at an FCA conference? Man, you've got to be kidding!

"The auditorium quiets. On the platform stands what appears to be a stage for a puppet show, connected by cables to an electronic panel.

"To the microphone strides a bespectacled, curly-haired, middle-aged man. Bill Leach looks as out of place as a salmon fisherman in the Sahara. 'Come with me to Jerusalem,' he says. 'Events are occurring which are rocking the countryside. We are going to tune in on the greatest story ever told as it might have been reported.'"

This is a scene from any of several FCA Camps and Conferences from the mid-1960s to the late 1970s as described by Gary Warner, former editor of *The Christian Athlete*. His article "The All-American Artist" told the story of a former Hollywood artist who became one of FCA's most influential speakers. Bill Leach used his artistic ability to bring the crucifixion to life on canvas for a captivated audience, and in the process, touched many lives.

"The first time I really heard the Gospel was at my first FCA Conference," said high school coach Billy Patton in a 1993 interview with Wayne Atcheson. "I saw artist Bill Leach draw a picture of the cross, and he played a tape that went along with that, kind of like a 'you are there' type of tape. I looked at that and for the first time in my life, I felt that God loved me."

Like many Christians, Bill Leach found Christ during troubled times.

In the late 1930s, Leach was working as a painter in the animation department of 20th Century Fox in Hollywood. Even though he was being paid to be an artist, Leach felt "complete emptiness" as he worked hard during the day and lived hard at night. But that all changed in 1939 when the studio was shut down by a strike.

"A friend and I hit skid row," Leach said. "We just drifted, spending all our money. One evening we wandered into the Union Rescue Mission. To eat we had to listen to a preacher. I wasn't about to do that, but I had to get some food."

Instead of a minister, the presentation was delivered by a youth group from the Hollywood Presbyterian Church.

"I expected them to scold us in a Sunday School way, but instead, a sharp, young guy rose and said, 'This is a faithful saying and worthy of all acceptation, that Christ Jesus came into the world to save sinners,'" Leach said. "That impressed me. I qualified."

After turning his life over to the Lord, Leach returned to work at Fox with a new passion to share his faith.

Years later, in 1961, former University of North Carolina basketball star Danny Lotz invited Leach to an FCA National Conference, where he presented the Gospel through his chalk art. Leach remained involved with the organization in various forms until his death in 1994.

Today, the legacy of Bill Leach lives on through his protégé, Ben Glenn, who began studying under Leach as an FCA intern. Glenn has continued to minister through chalk art, presenting to various groups, both Christian and secular, across the country.

"Bill was my friend, teacher and mentor," Glenn said. "He poured all he had into showing me how to continue the ministry of Living Art."✝

Bill Leach (with Kansas City Area Director John Shore, opposite) could make scenes come to life with a few pieces of chalk.

| Roger Bannister runs first sub-4-minute mile. | *Sports Illustrated* debuts. | President Dwight Eisenhower modifies the Pledge of Allegiance to include the phrase "under God." | *I Love Lucy*, *Dragnet* and *The Jackie Gleason Show* are tops on TV. | First TV sets are marketed for $1,000 each. | |

1955

| First McDonald's opens in Des Plaines, Illinois. | Disneyland opens. | Rosa Parks refuses to give up her seat on a bus to a white man in Montgomery, Ala., prompting a bus boycott by other African-Americans. | Weekly church attendance is estimated to be 49 million adults, roughly half of the nation's adult population. | The minimum wage is raised from 75 cents to $1.00. |

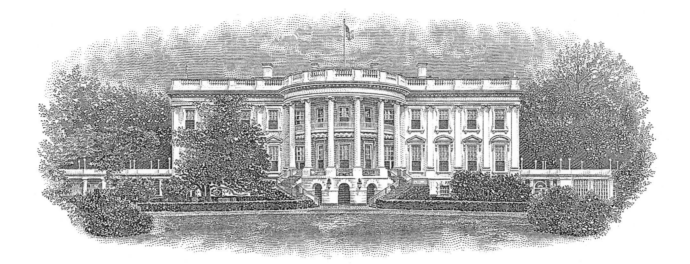

In the 'White' House of God

When FCA was invited to the White House on October 18, 1970, it was a very tense time in our nation, and doubly so at the Executive Mansion.

The Vietnam War was ablaze with intense fighting and bloodshed. All eyes of the world were on the White House as the war had intensified.

Six days after President Richard Nixon was sworn into office on January 20, 1969, he held his first worship service in the White House. "I feel that it is entirely in order to convert the great East Room—which has seen the making of so much American history—into a 'church' on Sunday mornings," President Nixon said. "It serves as an appropriate reminder that we feel God's presence here, and that we seek His guidance here—and that ours is, in the words of the Pledge of Allegiance, 'one nation, under God, indivisible...'"

President Nixon invited his friend, Rev. Billy Graham, to preach in the first White House worship service. Rev. Graham was followed by such men as Rev. Richard Halverson, Dr. Louis Evans, Dr. Norman Vincent Peale, Dr. Allan Watson and Dr. Elton Trueblood. All of these men had been key instruments in the founding years of FCA.

"Although I always make the final choice of the minister for each worship service, I do have some good help—for which I am most grateful," President Nixon said. "We have been truly honored by the presence of these devout and talented men, and I think most of them have felt honored to be at the White House."

FCA was in its 16th year when the invitation came from the White House to conduct a worship service there. At that time, it may have been the highest invitation and recognition FCA ever had received. It came just two weeks before the service. The small FCA staff (15 men) and the Board of Directors were included in the invitation. It was indeed a high honor and privilege for FCA, still growing and striving to reach the masses.

FCA staff members and their wives flew to Washington D.C. on Saturday morning, October 17. Board of Directors members came from across America.

The 20 people arrived the next morning at the security gate at the southwest corner of the White House. The worship hour was 11:15 a.m. in the East Room. FCA guests were directed into the historic room by Marine escorts and awaited the arrival of government officials and President and Mrs. Nixon.

The room was filled with 250 guests. A young Marine played hymns on the organ. There was a hushed reverence as the President and his wife walked in. ⇨

From left: Jay Wilkinson, John Erickson, Pat Nixon, President Nixon, Bobby Richardson and Rex Kern.

The President began by saying, "As always, we are delighted to have all of you here as guests at the White House worship service, and we think we have a highly unusual program this morning. This time, instead of asking some distinguished member of the clergy to conduct the service, we have turned to the world of sports."

He then proceeded to introduce John Erickson, Milwaukee Bucks vice president who was running for the U.S. Senate seat from Wisconsin and would have the opening prayer; Rex Kern, Ohio State senior quarterback who would read the Scripture; Jay Wilkinson, a former Duke All-American and a member of Congress who would give the benediction; and Bobby Richardson, a former Major leaguer who helped start Baseball Chapel and who would bring the message.

Kern, who had played a game for the Buckeyes the day before, read from 1 John 1: 1-7. Music was provided by the famous Danish Boys' Choir from Copenhagen, Denmark.

Richardson began his message by saying, "Ours is truly a sports-orientated society. I'm excited because I believe the Fellowship of Christian Athletes can be one of the greatest exponents of the Christian witness in our land." He explored with the President and his guests the story of the rich young ruler in Mark 10 and closed with the poem "God's Hall of Fame."

Guests spilled into the Red Room, China Room, Blue Room, Green Room and even into the family library. President and Mrs. Nixon greeted each of the FCA staff and Board members, and the other worshippers for well over an hour in the State Dining Room. The atmosphere was noticeably friendly and informal.

President and Mrs. Nixon repeatedly stressed that it was one of the most enjoyable worship services ever held at the White House. Julie Nixon-Eisenhower stated without reservation, "That was the best."

After the reception, President and Mrs. Nixon posed with the FCA staff and Board members for a memorable photograph. It was and still remains one of FCA's finest hours. ♱

Participating in the worship service at the Nixon White House was a highlight for the FCA staff and Board.

Making a Difference Through Abstinence

In 1985, a group of Dallas FCA area representatives sat down to a meeting that would change the nation. None of them knew it, but when Area Rep Kathy Golla first spoke the phrase "One way to play," it began a revolution in American drug prevention.

FCA Foundation President Carey Casey, also an area representative at the time, was at that meeting.

"We were sitting there trying to come up with a name for a program to deal with the drug problem in Dallas," Casey said. "We were there talking and she said, 'One way to play. What do you think?' And that's where the concept first came up."

The initial program, designed specifically for the Dallas area, asked participants to sign a drug-free commitment card. Once they signed up, they would receive an autographed card from Dallas Cowboys Coach Tom Landry, who was a major supporter of the program.

The program flourished in Dallas, but it wasn't until 1988, when Casey took a position at the FCA Home Office, that the program would be introduced on a national level.

"My title was National Urban Director, but under that title, I was also the drug-prevention coordinator," Casey said. "Anything we did with drugs and alcohol prevention was my responsibility. So we adopted *One Way 2 Play!* and it grew even deeper by going across the country."

The *OW2P!* program took another major step in 1994. Robert Plunk, former President and CEO of Preferred Risk Mutual Insurance Company and FCA ⇨

Former FCA Trustee Harvey Gainey embraced the OW2P! program,
placing decals on all his transportation Company trucks.

GAINEY TRANSPORTATION SERVICES, INC.

GRAND RAPIDS, MI

ONE WAY 2 PLAY

DRUG FREE

FAITH
COMMITMENT
ACCOUNTABILITY

1-800-289-0909

99004

Air Ride Equipp

GOD BLESS AMERICA!!

National Trustee, made a significant donation from his company to FCA, which was to be used toward the advancement of *OW2P!*

From there, the results have spoken for themselves.

To date, more than 260,000 people have signed commitment cards agreeing to play drug-free. A 1999 survey revealed that 63 percent of those who signed these cards were very successful at maintaining that commitment. Not one of the students surveyed said that they were not at all successful.

The impact of *OW2P!* on the youth of America has been so significant that the program even has drawn the attention of the White House. Vice President Dick Cheney, who visited the FCA Home Office in 2000, praised the program and FCA for its "position of leadership in the battle to restore character to America's schools and her youth."

With the success of the program, *OW2P!* undoubtedly will continue to be a cornerstone of FCA for many years to come. ✝

Attorney General John Ashcroft (above) recognizes the success of the OW2P! program becasue it's a hit with the kids.

| 1956 | Elvis Presley makes his debut on the charts. | Television remote control invented. | The Salk polio vaccine is marketed world-wide. | Don Larsen pitches only perfect game in World Series history. | American actress Grace Kelly marries Prince Rainier of Monaco. |

1957

The Soviet Union successfully launches Sputnik I, the first man-made object to orbit Earth.

Ford Motor Co. introduces the Edsel.

West Side Story opens on Broadway.

President Eisenhower sends Federal troops to uphold integration of schools in Little Rock, Ark.

The Brooklyn Dodgers and New York Giants move to Los Angeles and San Francisco, respectively.

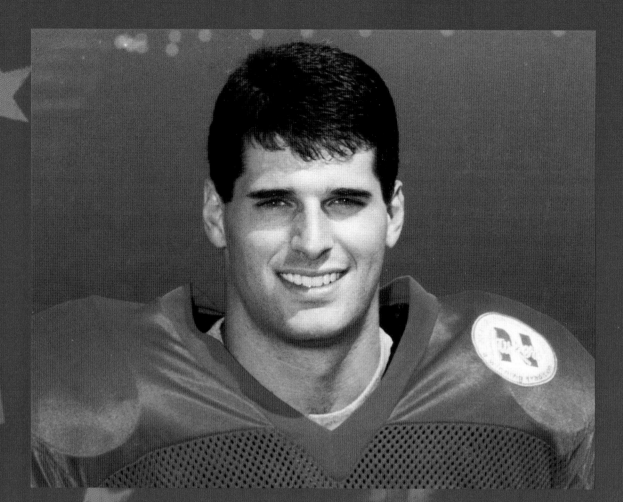

Faithful Follower

People die every day. "Good" people die every day. Maybe not every day, but the death of a prominent athlete—past or present—is not an uncommon occurrence either. So what was it about the death of Brook Berringer that brought an entire state to tears?

It wasn't his "tragic" death. It was his "triumphant" life.

Berringer was a four-year letter-winner for the University of Nebraska football team. He started a total of seven games in those four years, but it was what he did when he was not starting that impressed most people.

Following the 1994 season, when he started those seven games in place of injured starter Tommie Frazier and led the Cornhuskers to the national championship game, Berringer was relegated to the bench for the beginning of the 1995 season. Frazier's health was an issue in 1995 again, but this time Berringer got hurt and couldn't play either.

Instead of getting bitter, he accepted the decision and kept his positive approach to life.

Berringer's ability to transform the hurt of not starting, whether it was because of injury or just the coach's decision, was inspiring. He never moped. Instead, he spent his time in hospitals and schools, giving back to God by giving his life to others.

Two days before the 1996 NFL Draft, when Berringer was expected to be one of the first quarterbacks selected, he was traveling to speak at an FCA banquet. The plane he was piloting crashed in a hayfield. Berringer died in that crash.

The October 1996 issue of *Sharing the VICTORY* reported the following:

"In reporting his death, normally tough-minded sportscasters were moved to tears and sportswriters stumbled over a plethora of adjectives to describe the indescribable essence of who this sports star was."✞

Berringer impacted the fans with his play on the field and much more with his powerful testimony.

Giving Praise
Where Praise is Due

What do college football bowl games and church have in common? Both involve crowds of people, many of them raising their hands in praise and shouting their approval.

Taking the analogy one step further, FCA has sponsored breakfasts in conjunction with many of the season-ending bowl games for years. Both participating teams and their fans, plus football fans in the host city, are invited to share time, food and fellowship, plus solid teaching from the Word of God.

"This is a great opportunity for people in our community to see what FCA is doing for our young people," said Joe Oliver, who, as area director in South Florida, is in charge of the FCA Orange Bowl Breakfast. "Having the participating teams in attendance draws people who might not otherwise come. Once they're here, they get a first-hand experience of what the FCA ministry is all about."

The Orange Bowl Breakfast, sponsored by Ocean Bank, is the oldest and largest FCA bowl breakfast, but it's hardly the only one. In recent years, approximately two-thirds of the 20-plus bowl games had FCA breakfasts as part of the week's activities. Speakers range from former football players and coaches to well-known preachers to prominent politicians. In some cases, they're one in the same.

J.C. Watts is one former football standout who went on to a career in politics. He's also an ordained minister. Watts was a quarterback for the University of Oklahoma who led the Sooners to back-to-back Orange Bowl titles in 1980 and 1981. While serving as a U.S. Congressman from Oklahoma, Watts has spoken at several different bowl breakfasts through the years, including the Orange Bowl Breakfast in 2001, prior to

"This is a great opportunity for people in our community to see what FCA is doing for our young people."

—FCA Miami Director Joe Oliver

the BCS championship game between Florida State and his beloved Sooners.

"Joe Oliver called me and asked if I believed in free speech," Watts told the crowd of more than 2,000 people. "I said, 'I'm in the U.S. House of Representatives. Of course I do.' He then said, 'Good, I need one.'"

Many of the speakers donate their time in exchange for travel expenses, tickets to the game or simply the opportunity to share their love for Christ with those in attendance.

The Orange Bowl Breakfast was started in 1971 with 300 in attendance. It grew steadily until it plateaued at 900. In 1989, the idea to include local student-athletes increased attendance by 300. The community noticed and attendance has continued to rise, to an all-time high of 3,200 in 1995. The breakfast has averaged around 3,000 ever since.⇨

J.C. Watts (above) is one of many regular speakers at FCA bowl breakfasts, where hundreds—if not thousands—of fans gather to share a meal and hear the Word.

A staple of each breakfast are the testimonies delivered by the student-athletes representing each team. With FCA prominent on so many major college campuses, it's usually not a problem to find a player who is ready and willing to share his faith in Christ. Typically, many in the crowd will know about FCA. But many others will not.

When you see strong, young men on the cusp of a national championship stand up and say that their strength comes only from God, it is hard not to be moved.

FCA has used the term "influence" to summarize its ministry for most of its history. There are few examples any better than FCA bowl breakfasts to show that athletes and coaches have an influence on the world. ☦

Dr. Billy Graham (center) was one of the first-year visitors to the Alabama Huddle.

A Tide of Faith

Coach Paul "Bear" Bryant telephoned his good friend, Gene Stallings at Texas A&M, one fall day in the late 1960s and said, "Gene, do you know what is the worst thing that has happened to our football team?"

Coach Stallings on the other end responded, "What's that, Coach?" The answer from Coach Bryant came, "It's the Fellowship of Christian Athletes. These players are doing nothing but hugging on one another, loving on one another and they won't hit anybody."

At the end of what proved to be another banner year, he called Coach Stallings again. "Gene, do you know what is the best thing that has happened to our football team? It's the FCA. It has brought such a oneness and closeness to our team. We were unified because of the influence FCA has had on our team."

For 40 consecutive years, the FCA at Alabama has met every Wednesday night at 9 p.m. It is believed to be the longest-running college fellowship with consecutive weekly meetings in the nation. The group has had only four advisors. They have been Dr. Charlie Barnes (1964-73), Dr. Gary White (1973-85), Wayne Atcheson (1985-2002) and Jeremiah Castille (2003-present).

The first meeting was held in September 1964 with nine young men and a pastor. FCA was 10 years old. Among the nine young men present were Steve Sloan, Paul Crane and Richard Cole of the football team; Eddie King, a track athlete; and Atcheson, then a sports information graduate assistant.

The first-year FCA group had visits from Dr. Billy Graham and Bill Glass. Dr. Graham preached a one-night crusade meeting in Denny Stadium on April 26, 1965. He visited with the FCA leadership in the athletic dormitory that afternoon. Glass, an all-pro defensive end with the Cleveland Browns, spoke at an FCA meeting that spring.

Sloan and Crane were All-Americans as quarterback and center-linebacker respectfully. Their impact as standup Christians launched FCA at Alabama, and it was enhanced with national championships in 1964 and 1965.

Athletes were invited to speak in churches and to youth groups across the state. They gave invocations at Alabama athletic events. In the spring of 1966, Sloan gave his testimony at the Billy Graham Crusade in Greenville, S.C.

Weekly meetings drew in athletes from all sports. Women athletes joined the group in the mid-1970s. Beginning in 1964, Calvary Baptist Church pastor Allan Watson invited Coach Bryant and the football team to Squad Sunday as the season began. Some of the nation's most recognized athletes and coaches have spoken at Squad Sunday over the past 40 years at Calvary, one block from the stadium. One player has been selected each year for the Charlie Compton Award for outstanding Christian leadership. ⇨

In 1989, FCA was recognized at the Alabama/LSU football game for 25 years of Christian service on campus. Through the years, FCA has been led by some of the top players and most popular students on campus, such as John Croyle, Gary and Jeff Rutledge, Robert Fraley, Walter Lewis, Howard Cross, Alan Ward (longtime FCA rep in Birmingham), Steadman Shealy, Keith Pugh (former FCA state director for 10 years), Chad Goss, John David Phillips and Andy Phillips. Alabama head basketball coach Mark Gottfried met his wife, Elizabeth, at an FCA meeting. Many others have met their spouses at FCA as well.

When Coach Bryant died on January 26, 1983, FCA athletes served as his pallbearers. Ironically, the first FCA sponsor, Dr. Barnes, 90, passed away on the 40th Squad Sunday, August 17, 2003.

The 50-yard line post-game prayer began its tradition at Alabama in 1987. The first was after a hard-fought game at Penn State. Howard Cross was the instigator and even took the idea on into the NFL with the New York Giants. After the 1988 Sun Bowl game with Army, the entire Cadet team bowed with the Alabama players at midfield.

Two of Alabama's most visible Christian Athletes have been Jay Barker and Shaun Alexander. Before his sophomore year in 1992, Barker stood before 3,000 youth in Birmingham and said, "I'm Jay Barker, 6-4, 210-pound quarterback of the Alabama Crimson Tide. I have never had a drink of alcohol, have not taken any drugs and I'm a virgin."

Barker quarterbacked Alabama to the national championship that season and posted an incredible 35-2-1 career record as a starting quarterback. Yet, he was known more for his statement than his play on the field. Barker led the Alabama FCA group for three years.

✠

The 50-yard line post-game prayer began its tradition at Alabama in 1987. The first was after a hard-fought game at Penn State. Howard Cross was the instigator and even took the idea on into the NFL with the New York Giants.

✠

Alexander was cheered for scoring touchdowns on Saturday afternoons and being an All-American running back in 1999. Yet, on Wednesday nights at FCA, some 225 would pack the FCA meetings as Alexander turned into a cheerleader for Jesus. He would start every FCA meeting with the Jesus cheer. "Give me a J-E-S-U-S," Shaun would yell. "What do you got?" They would respond, "Jesus, Jesus, Jesus!"

FCA continues to have a mighty impact on the Alabama campus and throughout the state and region. It is a great part of the Alabama athletic tradition. Countless lives have received their salvation and eternal life because of athletes' boldness in witnessing for Jesus Christ, the Master Coach, on campus and beyond.

Faithful and consistent ministry to the FCA purpose for 40 years has been a glorious journey, and the impact will last for eternity. ✠

As big as football is at Alabama, it is down the list for members of the FCA Huddle like Alexander (top left).

A Product of the Ministry

Sue Kelly was not unlike many athletes her age. She wanted to win, and she didn't care how she did it. If she had to, she would step on toes, throw "'bows" or cheat in order to come out on top.

Growing up with two brothers and a twin sister to compete with in everything, she played sports all the time. She lived in New Jersey, and there was always a game to be played. There were no organized sports for girls in her junior high school, so she worked on her game on the playgrounds and driveways in her neighborhood.

Her family moved to Kansas City prior to her junior year of high school, where her street style of play gave her a starting spot on the varsity in basketball and softball.

She also found a sport new to her—volleyball. The coach noticed her jumping ability and athleticism and invited her to come out for the team. It ended up being the sport she would coach one day at the NCAA Division I level. It also played a role in Kelly meeting the One she would call her Savior.

She had never heard of the Fellowship of Christian Athletes, but her teammates invited her to attend the weekly meetings. She declined, but they persisted. Finally, they bribed her with tickets to a Kansas City Royals game on the condition she go to a Huddle meeting the next week, and she finally accepted.

She met Christian kids who "treated me nice for no particular reason," she said. She was invited to her first party without alcohol and found out it was "way more fun than those with alcohol."

The Huddle at Shawnee Mission South High School was very active with regular student-led discussions, evening activities, and involvement at Camps and rallies, so she started attending.

The mission of FCA is "to present to athletes and coaches the challenge and adventure of receiving Jesus Christ as Savior and Lord, serving him in their relationships and in the fellowship of the church."

FCA was all that to Kelly. She was the athlete, influenced by her fellow athletes, who saw the challenge and adventure of serving Christ through her Christian friends. A year after going to her first FCA event, after a Huddle meeting where a college wrestler explained the real meaning of the cross, Kelly accepted Jesus Christ as her Savior.

"I listened to that wrestler tell a story I had heard from childhood, but he told it with tears running down his face," she said. "He was big and tough, but the fact that Jesus gave His life to make a way for all of us to know His Father broke his heart. For weeks afterward, I couldn't get the picture of Jesus dying for me out of my head, and I finally knelt in a quiet place and asked Him to be Lord of my life."

She had grown up an angry athlete. She wondered why things didn't go her way, even if she gave what she thought was her best. "I did not understand competition," she said. "I wanted to win, and I didn't care how."

With her new-found faith in Christ, she learned to turn the results over to God. "Romans 8:28—'And we know that in all things God works for the good of those who love him, who have been called according to his purpose'—became my verse," she said. "I learned to let go of my control and let God be in control."

After high school, Kelly attended Bethany College in Lindsborg, Kan., where she lettered and won all-conference honors in volleyball, basketball, softball and track. She was all-district in basketball and district champ in the javelin and even made the Olympic "B" team in team handball.

Her senior year she was named Bethany College Female Athlete of the Year and also Kansas FCA Female College Athlete of the Year. Ten years later (in 1993), she became the first female athlete to be inducted into the Bethany College Hall of Honor.

She went into coaching and spent two years at the high school level, and then God unexpectedly opened a door for her to become a head college coach at the age of 23. Finding herself in a dream job at the NCAA Division I level, she began to struggle with two things.⇨

Alaska becomes a state.

Pope John XXIII is elected.

An Oldsmobile may be purchased for $2,933.

Pan American Airlines launches trans-Atlantic jet service.

U.S. launches first satellite into orbit.

"After five years of success, the next three years were very difficult. After taking a new job at a more prestigious university, I felt like I was being asked to compromise my Christian principles," she said. She also was reminded of a vow she had made to the Lord 10 years earlier.

She found an old journal, written when she was in college, that read: "Ten years after I graduate from college, if God wants me in sports missions, I will go."

Confirmation came shortly thereafter when the FCA female staff member in St. Louis told her that she was moving and suggested that Kelly pray about being a "home missionary" with FCA right there. She served in St. Louis and in Oregon before taking her current role as area director in central Pennsylvania.

It's a natural fit for Kelly. She's near her old stomping ground, though she's traveled enough with her various jobs that there's a little bit of home in nearly every state. And she's doing what she never would have dreamed of doing before her junior year of high school, but something for which she's a natural.

"I'm thrilled that every day I get a chance to combine my two greatest passions—sharing Christ and sports."

Kelly is one of approximately 600 FCA staff members who share the vision to "impact the world for Jesus Christ through the influence of athletes and coaches." Like many of her colleagues, she's also a product of the ministry. ✞

Kelly (left) has spent her adult life focused on introducing kids to Christ.

1959

| Fidel Castro takes power in Cuba. | Hawaii becomes the 50th state. | Eighty-six percent of the American population owns a television set. | St. Lawrence Seaway opens allowing ocean ships to reach the Midwest from the Atlantic. | Rock 'n roll stars Buddy Holly and Ritchie Valens are killed in a plane crash. |

Spreading the Word in School

The faculty and staff members at Citrus High School in Inverness, Fla., got quite a surprise when they came to work on December 20, 2002. In each of the staff mailboxes was a gift-wrapped Bible, courtesy of the high school's FCA Huddle. Each Bible was engraved with the staff member's name, and contained a hand-written note from the Huddle members, which read:

"This Christmas season, you have been thought of by Christian students within your school known as FCA—Fellowship of Christian Athletes. This Bible is a gift to you from us out of love, much like Jesus' gift to us on the cross. This Christmas, we hope and pray that you will receive the ultimate gift, which is found within the covers of this book. We hope you will find your way this Christmas."

The response to the gift was overwhelming. Teachers flooded the Huddle members and their coach, Rick Keeran, with thank you cards and e-mails. In fact, out of the 168 Bibles that were distributed, only one was returned.

"It wasn't the fact that this person didn't want it," Keeran said, "but they had a problem with the fact that the administration let us do it to begin with. The administration told them that it was student-led, and they couldn't stop it."

The idea for the Bible distribution came from then Huddle President Mike Wilburn, a 2002 graduate of Citrus High School.

"It wasn't anything that we had seen before," Wilburn said. "It was just something that a couple of us thought of—something that we wanted to do before we graduated."

The process of raising the $6,000 needed for the Bibles took more than a year. The Huddle held a car wash at a local car dealership, solicited donations from churches and received numerous contributions from individuals in the community.

After the money had been raised and the Bibles had been purchased, the Huddle members gathered at Wilburn's house to gift-wrap the Bibles and to write the notes.

"We talked about typing the letter, but the more we discussed it, the more we thought that it would be more personal if we wrote it," Keeran said. "They actually wrote all the words on the letters and signed them by hand."

There was, however, a slight apprehension among several of the Huddle members as to how the Bibles would be received by the faculty.

"I told them that they might have some teachers who might be upset with it, and that if they were upset with it, not to let it bother them," Keeran said. "I said, 'If God's in it, it's going to happen whether they want it to or not.'"✝

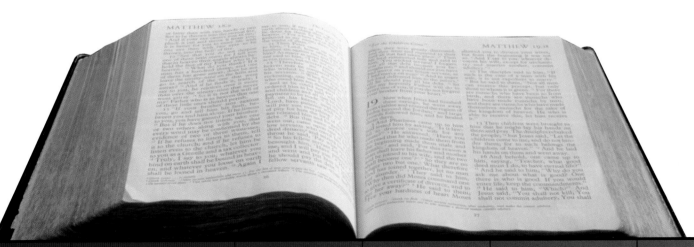

1960

| Wilma Rudolph becomes first American woman to win three track and field Olympic gold medals. | A U.S. spy plane is shot down over the Soviet Union; pilot Gary Powers is captured. | Sen. John F. Kennedy is elected president. | The laser is invented by Theodore Maiman. | Berry Gordy starts Motown Records with an $800 loan. |

2002-03 Citrus High School Huddle

1961

Roger Maris hits his 61st home run, breaking Babe Ruth's 34-year old record.

Alan Shepard becomes the first American in space.

President Kennedy establishes the goal of landing a man on the moon by the end of the decade.

East Germany erects the Berlin Wall.

Chubby Checker launches the "twist" craze.

Twirling Fancy

Tonya Crevier has spun more basketballs at one time than many people can spin in a lifetime. As the renowned "world's greatest female basketball handler," Crevier has entertained countless thousands of people and left them thinking, "How can she keep so many balls spinning at one time?"—both literally and figuratively.

Crevier will spin one ball on each hand, one on a stick that she holds between her teeth, one on each foot, and four others on sticks that are attached one way or another to her legs. And she does it nearly every day of the year, in all parts of the world.

"I don't even touch a basketball until I read my Bible," she says of her routine. "Basketball used to take precedence over my relationship with God. It's powerful when you start each day by asking God to speak through His Word. There may be things in your life that have taken priority over your relationship with God. He will show us graciously, or He'll show us not so graciously."

For more than 22 years, Crevier has traveled around the country giving demonstrations at FCA-sponsored events, such as school rallies. She also participates in prison ministry. And she has traveled overseas on numerous occasions as well with her message of teamwork, commitment to goals and maintaining a good attitude.

But it's when she mentions the source of her strength and motivation—her relationship with Christ—that she has the biggest impact.

"When your foundation is built on the Gospel of Jesus Christ, then you know there is a supernatural Power working through you," Crevier says. "I see kids and adults alike who are paying the price for the wrong decisions they have made. I'm then able to share with the kids how people in prison ask me to tell the kids to stay away from drugs, alcohol and immorality.

"Maybe there are kids who are on the edge, experimenting with this stuff, thinking, 'Should I or should I not?' You trust that God sent you there for those kids, that the Holy Spirit will convict them of their need to repent."

Crevier generally uses helpers at her performances. She'll ask one of the kids to come forward and she spins a ball or two before giving it to the child and showing him or her how to keep it spinning. Often she picks the person in the crowd who needs encouragement the most.

"I just pray before each assembly that the Lord lets me be His voice, hands and feet to touch people," she says. "Kids need a touch of God. Whether it's going to be through an FCA meeting, youth group or school assembly, God can move in powerful ways."

It's enough to make your head or, more appropriately, a few basketballs spin. ✝

Find Tonya Crevier and you'll likely find a basketball—or several of them—entertaining somebody.

"Jesus looked at them and said,
'With man this is impossible,
but not with God; all things
are possible with God.'"
—Mark 10:27

CHALLENGE

Challenge

Off to a Quick Start

When FCA organized its first Conference (Camp), there was some doubt as to whether the idea would fly. Would athletes and coaches around the country be willing to travel to little Estes Park, Colo., for the sake of gathering for a Christian sports camp?

The answer was a resounding yes, as a "Who's Who" in college and professional sports were among the 256 attendees in August 1956.

FCA rallies had been a big success and were gathering momentum. Requests for athletes to share their faith were stacking up in FCA's headquarters in Norman, Okla. There were many new ideas for ministry bouncing around, and FCA President Don McClanen felt compelled to share the one about a sports camp with Dr. Louis Evans, a prominent Presbyterian minister and chaplain of the U.S. Senate, and an integral part of the early years of FCA.

Evans invited McClanen to attend a week at the YMCA of the Rockies in the spring of 1956. It didn't take long for them to choose that spot for the first FCA Camp. It

was scheduled for August 19-23, and McClanen optimistically planned for an enrollment of 500. The plans did not take off, however, and one month before the Camp was to begin, there were "reservations," because there weren't enough reservations.

The big boost came in a July *Guideposts* article on Robin Roberts that mentioned the upcoming Camp. It mentioned that FCA would host its first Conference and that famous sports personalities such as Cleveland Browns Hall of Fame quarterback Otto Graham, 1948 Heisman Trophy winner Doak Walker and baseball legend Branch Rickey would be there. It also gave FCA's headquarters contact information. The article may have been the first use of the now-famous tagline for FCA Camps—"inspiration and perspiration."

Two hundred and fifty-six athletes and coaches arrived on August 19 and were treated to a smorgasbord of sports celebrities. Graham was in charge of the football clinics, assisted by Walker. Rickey was in charge of baseball, assisted by former major league pitcher Frank Hiller. University of Kansas ⇨

basketball coach Phog Allen was in charge of basketball. There even were clinics for sports broadcasters and sportswriters.

Some of the other Huddle "Captains" and clinicians were Rafer Johnson, world record holder and 1956 Olympic silver medallist in the decathlon; Donn Moomaw, All-American football player at UCLA; "Biggie" Munn, legendary athletic director at Michigan State University; major-league pitchers Roberts and Dave "Boo" Ferris; and future FCA staffers Bill Krisher, Ron Morris, James Jeffrey and Gary Demarest.

Demarest was the first Camp dean. One of his tasks was to pick up Rickey at the Denver airport. "We wondered whether our dreams would become a reality," Demarest recalled later. "Branch Rickey consoled me with, 'Don't forget, Jesus started with 12!' Almost all of the 256 were there that night when Mr. Rickey gave the keynote message."

Rickey spoke for more than 50 minutes, not so much about his baseball career, but about his Christian heritage. He was the man who had integrated major league baseball with the signing of Jackie Robinson.

He also had played for four years (1904-07) and managed for 10 (1913-15, 1919-25). But he spoke about the promise he made to his parents to "honor the Sabbath" (see his story, page 104) and the importance of athletics.

"It is an integral part of our nation. We could hardly get along without it. It's so meaningful. Our language is continuously filled with it. Illustrations in the ministry and even in the field of statesmanship constantly use and understand it."

Rickey was clear about his relationship with Christ. "Jesus is not a myth. He's not a fraud. He's not the plausible but illogical philosopher," he said. "He's the Light of the world. He is to me."

The schedule, planned by McClanen, Moomaw and Demarest, is very similar to the one still used in FCA Camps today. Rise and shine was at 6:30 a.m., followed by chapel at 6:45, breakfast at 7:15 and devotional time at 8 a.m. Assembly went from 8:30 to 10:30, with a break from 9:15 to 9:30. Huddle time was at 10:45 and lunch followed at 11:45. ⇨

More than 250 athletes and coaches gathered at the first Conference, where Branch Rickey gave the keynote message.

In the afternoon, coaches and professional athletes gave "chalk-talks" and lectures, followed by demonstrations and clinics. There was free time from 3:30 to 6 p.m., then they ate dinner. The evening assembly was at 7:30, with Huddle meetings from 9:30 to 10:30. Lights out was at 11 p.m.

The Camp was not only big news for FCA, it was national news. *Life*, *Newsweek* and *Sports Illustrated* covered the Camp, and even President Dwight D. Eisenhower and Secretary of State John Foster Dulles sent telegrams to be read by Dr. Evans.

"The 1956 Estes Park National Camp may have been the most important event in the history of the Fellowship of Christian Athletes," Wayne Atcheson wrote in his 1994 book, *Impact for Christ*. "The infant movement had attracted many of the top men in American sports at that time. It was the first meeting of its kind with sports enthusiasts gathering in the name of Jesus Christ to spark a movement. Only God could measure the results from that week on.

"Branch Rickey said on his drive to the Camp that Jesus started with 12 men. It could be said that FCA started with 256 men that would spread the message and Gospel of Jesus Christ through the influence of athletics and hero-worship as we know it today.

"This Camp brought together enormous strength from individuals of all levels of athletics. The powerful platform and vision in sharing what they had experienced is still vibrantly alive." ✝

The style of clothing may have changed since 1956, but the activities remain very similar in today's Camps.

"Jesus started with 12 men.
　　　　　　　It could be said that FCA started with 256 men."

A Light Through the Darkness.

On September 11, 2001, the world was changed forever. No one will forget the terrifying images of airplanes crashing into the towers of the World Trade Center and into the United States Pentagon.

It was on that day that FCA lost a very dear friend— Al Braca.

† † †

On the morning of September 11, Jeannie Braca switched on the television to check the weather report. Instead of hearing the local forecast, however, she learned the terrible news that a plane had struck the World Trade Center.

Jeannie's husband Al worked on the 105th floor of Tower One as a corporate bond trader for Cantor Fitzgerald. She hadn't spoken to him since he had left for work that morning.

"Normally we would talk on the phone a lot — maybe five or 10 times a day. We would pray together all the time, as different situations came up," Jeannie said.

The phone did begin to ring, but it wasn't Al. Anxious friends and relatives were calling to see if Jeannie had heard from her husband. Many of them made their way to the Braca home to offer support. They worried that the stress would be too much for Jeannie to handle, as a previous heart attack had left only 16 percent of her heart functioning.

When the second plane hit, they turned off the television. Jeannie was, in fact, starting to feel ill and having difficulty breathing. They didn't tell her when they heard that the towers had collapsed.

Later in the evening, after Jeannie had received medical treatment, her sons broke the news about the towers. Family members held out hope that Al only had been injured. They called area hospitals, searching for him, but Jeannie said, "By the time I went to bed that night, I knew he was never coming home."

A week later, Al's body was found in the rubble.

As reports trickled in from friends and acquaintances, the Bracas learned that Al had been ministering to people during the attack. When he realized that they were all trapped in the building and would not be able to escape, Al shared the Gospel with a group of 50 co-workers and led them in prayer.

This came as no surprise to his family and friends who knew that Al was born with the gift of evangelism and had a tremendous heart for other people.

Former FCA National Board of Trustees Chairman Gary Cuozzo said, "Al was a bigger-than-life kind of person. He was full of joy, fun to be with, always looking to live life to the fullest. He was a great husband, a great father and a great example to other people. He loved the Lord with all his heart and mind and soul, just as the Scriptures say. He lived to serve the Lord."

Through his friendship with FCA New Jersey Director Harry Flaherty, Al became involved in the support of the local FCA chapter, eventually serving as the chair of the local board. Jeannie says Al loved the ministry's unique ability to reach young people with the life-changing truths of the Gospel. ☩

Jeannie Braca says that Al witnessed to many of his co-workers, especially after the planes hit the World Trade Center.

U.S. Supreme Court decision outlaws state-sponsored prayer in public schools.

"Buck" O'Neil becomes first African-American to coach in Major League Baseball (Cubs).

John Glenn and his Mercury spacecraft Friendship 7 orbit Earth three times.

Wilt Chamberlain scores 100 points in an NBA game.

The Beverly Hillbillies and *The Dick Van Dyke Show* are TV hits.

| Lawrence of Arabia wins Best Picture at the Academy Awards | Martin Luther King, Jr. delivers his "I Have a Dream" speech. | President John Kennedy is assassinated. | Arthur Ashe becomes the first African-American to play on U.S. Davis Cup team. | Mickey Mantle hits a home run that would have traveled 620 feet if it hadn't hit the facade in Yankee Stadium, the longest home run in major league history. |

1963

Setting a Standard

Professional Christian athletes were critical role-players in the early years of FCA, and founder Don McClanen identified only a short list at the outset.

However, some of the nation's household names, such as Carl Erskine, Otto Graham, Robin Roberts, Alvin Dark, Dan Towler, Doak Walker, Bob Feller, George Kell, Vernon Law and Kyle Rote, Sr., provided the clout that helped to launch the Fellowship of Christian Athletes in the mid-1950s.

They already were endorsing shaving cream, razor blades and other products in magazines, on billboards, on radio and on a new phenomenon, television. "Hero worship" was a widely used term in the early FCA years. Until FCA was founded, it was rare to hear a professional athlete express his or her faith in Jesus Christ. The Christian athlete was a strange breed, seldom heard or found. His or her spiritual life was considered private.

One of the earliest known Christian witnesses involved Brooklyn Dodgers All-Star pitcher Carl Erskine. "In 1952, I pitched a no-hitter and Len LeSourd of *Guideposts* magazine came to our home, did an interview and wrote a story called 'The Inside Pitch.' Don McClanen evidently saw the article and saved it. Two years later, he approached me in Philadelphia and gave me this real brief idea about having athletes endorse their church life and Christian faith," Erskine remembers.

"I told Don right then, 'Yeah, I'll be glad to try that.' I'd not done that much before, but I told him, 'Yes, I think this will work.'"

God began to open doors and the hearts of dozens of male pro athletes who played vital roles in demonstrating their unashamed faith in Jesus Christ. Christians across the country were overjoyed and ⇨

Professional athletes such as Carl Erskine (above) and Bill Krisher (right) helped the FCA "movement" gain instant credibility.

thrilled to hear their heroes express their Christian faith in their sport and in their daily lives.

In the 1960s, the names included such men as Bill Glass, Raymond Berry, Bob Pettit, Bill Wade, Bobby Richardson, Bart Starr, Carroll Dale, Jerry Stovall, Prentice Gautt, Bill Bradley, Fran Tarkenton, Johnny Baker, Tony Romeo, Don Shinnick, Jim Ray Smith, Al Worthington, Jim Kaat, Bill Curry, Bobby Mitchell, Cazzie Russell, Gary Cuozzo and Jerry Kindall.

Many of these professional athletes served as pseudo staff in their areas. They arranged speakers for Huddles, did much of the speaking themselves and worked FCA's Camps.

One such professional was Shinnick of the Baltimore Colts. During his career, he spoke at countless ⇨

Athletes from many different sports jumped on board early.
Clockwise from lower left: "Deacon Dan" Towler,
Roger Staubach, Bob Pettit, Kyle Rote, Jr., and Rafer Johnson.

Huddles and Camps. He came up with the idea of competition at Camps. He called them the "Dogpatch Olympics," a tradition that continues in many Camps today.

Shinnick was chosen as FCA's first Pro Athlete of the Year in 1970. He also wrote a book that year called *Always a Winner*, and donated all the proceeds to FCA.

Following his playing career, he went into coaching at both the college and pro levels, but he never forgot his connection with FCA. He was inducted into the FCA Hall of Champions in 1999.

These men and a host of others gave themselves to the movement and began to attend FCA Camps and speak at FCA events across America. Their powerful impact led to thousands of new believers and gave even more the courage to stand for Christ.

The earliest pro chapel services were started by Glass with the Cleveland Browns, Berry and Shinnick of the Colts, and Dale of the Green Bay Packers. Their boldness has led every professional football, basketball and baseball team (major and minor leagues) today not only to have chapel programs but to have weekly Bible studies and team chaplains who minister on a daily basis.

These testimonies showed that athletes could be highly competitive on the playing field and also be Christians. Miami Dolphins lineman Norm Evans said of Houston Oiler Johnny Baker, "He was a solid

Christian and a furious linebacker who would break a quarterback's jaw on Sunday and visit him in the hospital on Monday."

In the early 1970s, quarterback Roger Staubach of the Dallas Cowboys became one of FCA's most celebrated role models. In FCA's first 50 years, no other pro athlete was as much in demand as a speaker as Staubach. He made hundreds of appearances and God used him mightily as the Cowboys became "America's Team" with Coach Tom Landry at the helm.

As FCA soared in the 1970s, pro athletes continued to have a profound impact. New names on the scene included Brooks Robinson, Tim Foley, Kyle Rote, Jr., Don Kessinger, Mike McCoy, Paul Crane, Winston Hill, Mike Kolen, Bob Vogel, Steve Owens, Jim Hart, Jerry Mays, Dan Reeves, Pettis Norman, Wally Armstrong, Kermit Zarley, Bert Yancey, Don Cockroft, Ralph Drollinger, Fred Cox and Kent Krammer, among many faithful and willing servants.

Bill Krisher, a professional football player who joined the FCA staff in its infancy, proclaims the pro athlete "a crucial ingredient to the success of the beginning years. Their power and impact provided the movement instant recognition and credibility. They also opened doors financially. The movement couldn't have blossomed without their involvement and willingness to serve." ✝

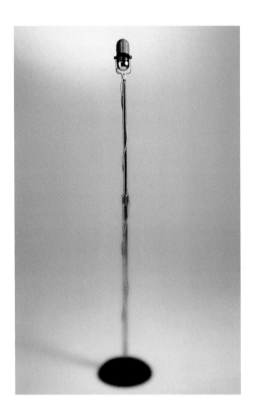

He Gave His Whole Life to Christ

There was a young man at an FCA Camp in Kutztown, Pa. The guys in his Huddle knew that "Rick" came from the mean streets of Washington D.C., but they didn't know how rough his life was.

It wasn't that he was poor. In fact, "Rick" had more "things" at his disposal than probably anybody in the Camp. It wasn't that he didn't have a role model. He had followed his brothers' footsteps quite closely. It wasn't that he didn't have direction. His future was well-defined.

"Rick" was a member of a street gang.

On Wednesday evening of that Camp, he accepted Jesus Christ as his Lord and Savior. He knew that it would mean a change in his life more drastic than for any of his fellow campers who might make the same decision.

At "Open Mic" on Thursday, "Rick" waited his turn. When he reached the front of the line, he told the severity of his commitment, "Yesterday, I accepted Jesus Christ as my Lord and Savior," he related. "He is Lord of my entire life. Everything I have, I give to Him.

"I am in a gang, and I am expected to stay in that gang for as long as I live. I won't do that, because it does not honor Jesus. I may not be alive at the end of this weekend, after I tell the gang that I am giving up this lifestyle. But that's okay, because I gave my whole life to Him."

The powerful influence of teammates and coaches cannot be understated. His fellow campers showed him that a relationship with Jesus Christ is more valuable than any job or possession on Earth, even more than life itself.

"For to me, to live is Christ and to die is gain." (Philippians 1:21)✝

Jim Ryun becomes the first high school athlete to run a sub-4-minute mile.

The Surgeon General declares that cigarette smoking causes lung cancer.

Cassius Clay (he later changed his name to Muhammed Ali) stops heavyweight champion Sonny Liston.

The Beatles appear on the *Ed Sullivan Show*.

Pop-Tarts are introduced to the American breakfast table.

1965

First U.S. combat troops are sent to Vietnam.

"What the World Needs Now is Love" is a hit song.

Bert Campanaris of the Kansas City Athletics becomes the first Major Leaguer to play all nine positions in one game.

The Mariner spacecraft flies by Mars and sends back snapshots.

Gateway Arch is completed in St. Louis.

Faithful to a Faithful God

Tom Cross has been faithful to FCA for so long that the parents of some of the kids he coaches today were not born yet when he first got involved.

In the summer of 1958, Cross was coaching football in Phillipsburg, Kan., when a local businessman heard about the FCA "movement" and a Conference (Camp) that was held in Estes Park, Colo. He paid for Cross and four student-athletes to attend the Camp, and Cross found the ministry to be right up his alley.

He has been involved in FCA ever since. He hasn't gone to Camp every year, but he's missed very few years. He's spoken at Camps, been a clinician at Camps and been a Huddle Coach at various schools.

"I'm not a big-time speaker," he said. "I speak at the small-time events."

He and his wife, June, also have been regular contributors to the ministry since the fall of 1960.

"If we missed a month (in giving), we doubled up the next month," Cross said. "We serve a faithful God."

Cross was influenced by Elton Trueblood at the FCA Camp in Lake Geneva, Wisc., in August 1960. Trueblood was the coaches' Huddle leader.

"He kept saying, 'You can tell what a man really believes by examining his checkbook.' I said, 'By golly, we better look at that checkbook.'"

Cross is in his seventh year as the strength coach for Mid-America Nazarene University in Olathe, Kan., and his 50th year in coaching overall. He has collected many memories of his involvement in athletics and FCA.

"Just hearing idols of mine that I have heard speak at various events has been great," he said. "I've taken something from every one of them. It's things like focusing on God and family, faithfulness, hard work, and striving to get better. That's what I believe in and what I'm trying my best to do.

"There are still a few other things that I would kind of like to do. But I will always be involved in FCA. It's about faithfulness. It's not about X's and O's, it's not about how much weight you can lift. It's about dealing with young people. I give out a lot of free advice, and every once in a while something neat happens. If I had to quit going around athletes, I wouldn't last very long."

Don't look for Cross to quit being around athletes any time soon. It's the only thing he's known and the only thing he wants to do for a living.

"I'm too old to look for honest work," he says, "so I'm just going to keep on doing this."

And as for his checkbook? Go ahead and examine it. It will show you that he really believes in FCA. ✞

Cross when he and FCA were younger (right), and today.

All-black Texas Western defeats all-white Kentucky in the NCAA men's basketball championship.

Frank Robinson wins the Triple Crown (hitting, home runs, RBIs); the most recent player in Major Leagues.

First U.S.-manned space flights launched.

Scientist Har Gobind Khorana deciphers the DNA code.

Star Trek, Batman and *Mission: Impossible* all make their debuts on TV.

196

| The first Super Bowl is played to a less-than-capacity crowd in Los Angeles. | Astronauts Grissom, Chaffee and White are killed in a fire in an Apollo test capsule. | Thurgood Marshall is appointed to the Supreme Court. | Dr. Christiaan Barnard performs the first heart transplant in South Africa. | The Beatles release their album "Sgt. Pepper's Lonely Hearts Club Band." |

Did 'Juneau' That FCA is in Alaska?

Adult Huddles have long been an integral part of the FCA ministry. They provide much-needed support and encouragement to student-athletes and coaches, and to the community itself. But when that community is hidden between a mountain range and the edge of a sea and has little interaction with the outside world, those roles are magnified significantly.

The FCA Huddle at Juneau-Douglas High School in Juneau, Alaska, came into being in the early 1990s when returning college students wanted to start a local Bible study and decided that FCA was the track they wanted to follow.

With their daughter, Sarah, became involved in the Bible study, Roger and Lee Kolden began heading up the Huddle and the Adult Chapter. When their son, Christian, reached high school age, he was heavily involved in sports, thus the Koldens became heavily involved in the day-to-day activities of the Huddle.

"We felt a real need for ministry to youth, and especially youth who aren't covered by a youth group that's associated with a church," Roger Kolden said. "Also, it's just nice to be able to help out some of the youth directors in town with a program that allows them to bring their kids. They don't have to plan it. They can sit back and enjoy it and watch it happen."

In an area where the high school football team has to be flown to all of its away games, the cost of running a local FCA can be a major issue.

The Adult Chapter holds only one fund-raiser a year—a golf tournament that raises approximately $500. The rest of the funds are donated by individuals.

That money goes in part to the Chapter's major investment: sending students to FCA Leadership Camp. "They send as many as 10 kids to Camp each summer," former FCA Western Division Vice President Jim Garner said. "That requires a pretty good investment, just for the airfare."

But Roger Kolden says the Chapter is not just doing it to be nice.

"Those kids provide the energy, coming back into the Huddle to run the program," he said. "They're the leaders."

He is confident that FCA will remain strong in the Juneau area long after he and his wife are out of the picture.

"There are good people out there who will pick up the slack," he said. "And of course, we realize that this is the Lord's ministry." ☩

1968

Bob Beamon breaks the long jump world record by nearly two feet.

Martin Luther King, Jr. is assassinated in Memphis.

St. Louis Cardinals pitcher Bob Gibson sets modern-day record with 1.12 ERA for the season.

Richard Nixon is elected President.

"Heidi" game takes place between New York Jets and Oakland Raiders.

Juneau, Alaska, is land-locked, but that doesn't keep the kids at Juneau-Douglas High School from having an FCA Huddle.

1969

"Miracle Mets" win World Series over Baltimore Orioles.

Astronaut Neil Armstrong is the first human to step foot on the Moon.

First regular-season baseball game is played outside the U.S. as Montreal defeats St. Louis, 8-7.

Chemical Bank in New York City is the first to install an automated teller machine (ATM).

Joe Namath delivers on "guarantee" and the Jets beat the Colts in Super Bowl III.

West Virginia Pioneers

The year was 1959. The Los Angeles Dodgers won the World Series, Alaska and Hawaii became states, the post-war baby boom was in full swing, and a man named Bill Smith was about to begin a lifelong journey with the Fellowship of Christian Athletes.

A good friend of Smith's, John Thomas, had captured his attention with a new project. Thomas was working to bring a growing ministry called FCA to his home state of West Virginia. Although not a Christian, Smith liked young people and the idea of promoting wholesome fellowship among student-athletes. He threw himself into Thomas' venture by volunteering his services to help establish West Virginia's FCA program.

The team laid the groundwork for the week-long campaign that would introduce FCA to the capitol city of Charleston. Activities were planned for schools and churches, speakers were arranged, and rallies and banquets were scheduled.

Smith's assignment for the campaign was to serve as an escort for Bill Wade, who was quarterback for the Los Angeles Rams at the time. He chauffeured Wade to the various events, all the while listening to the great athlete talk about Christ and watching him as he promoted FCA. After Wade had returned home, something unexpected happened to Bill Smith.

He got saved.

"I was not much of an athlete, and I wasn't a Christian. I guess I was strong on the 'fellowship' part of FCA," Smith said. "Maybe I was searching, but something led me to get involved. A day or two after Bill Wade left, I turned my life over to Jesus."

Before long, Smith's wife, Barbara, also became a Christian. They have been cornerstones of West Virginia's FCA program ever since.

"It's been his first love for years—young people and what they can do through athletics."

"It's been his first love for years—young people and what they can do through athletics," said Barbara, without complaint. "He won't tell you a whole lot. He's a very modest person. But I'm proud of him. He's a good Christian man who's done a lot of good, although he'd never say so."

Smith's participation has been instrumental to the development of FCA in West Virginia. He has served on the state board from its inception, often as president. He has attended numerous national and state Conferences and Camps, and has worked diligently in his local Adult Chapter.

He and Barbara also have supported the FCA financially.

"From the contributor's point of view, one of the biggest selling points of FCA, other than our mission, is that you get more bang for your buck than any dollar you give anywhere else, because most of the work is done by volunteers," Smith said.

Barbara agrees, "What [FCA] does with its money is phenomenal. People give their time, and we don't have to pay them to get everything done. In so many volunteer organizations, the money gets used up. We've always felt good about giving money to FCA because we know the money is well-spent. [The money] is used where it should be used—to benefit the kids."

When looking back on nearly a half-century of ministry, how would Smith like to be remembered?

"I don't care if I'm remembered or not," he said, "but I hope FCA will be remembered." ✞

Kansas City Chiefs win Super Bowl IV over Minnesota Vikings.

Willis Reed limps out of the locker room to help the New York Knicks win their first NBA championship.

Four students are killed at Kent State University in Ohio by National Guardsmen during an anti-war demonstration.

Monday Night Football makes its debut.

Diane Crump is the first female jockey to race in the Kentucky Derby.

"*Whatever you do, work at it with all your heart,
as working for the Lord, not for men.*"

—*Colossians 3:23*

| 1971 | First World Series night game played (Baltimore vs. Pittsburgh). | A ping-pong team from the United States competes in Communist China. | The U.S. voting age is lowered to 18. | *Brian's Song* is a hit TV movie. | The Beatles break up. | |

What's in a Name?

How do you get people to give large amounts of money to a worthy cause? That was the challenge for Ron Morris, FCA's vice president for special projects in 1980. He knew that FCA would struggle financially if it relied exclusively on lots of small gifts.

So he came up with a plan to start a major-donor program with incentives to give beyond the simple joy of blessing a ministry. FCA would have a program to which donors who gave more than $10,000 in a given year would belong. He also thought to name it the Tom Landry Associates, after the coach of the Dallas Cowboys who was such a visible leader of the ministry as a member and chairman of the Board of Trustees.

Morris and Landry were traveling to meet a potential donor in the early 1980s when Morris sprung the idea on Landry. "Coach, I would like to begin a new level of giving for FCA," Morris told Landry. "We would like to name it after you."

Landry thought the donor program was a good idea, but he could not see how his name would inspire anyone to give an extra dime. Morris reached into his jacket pocket and pulled out three checks for $10,000 made out to the Tom Landry Associates. The amazed Landry humbly agreed to lend his name.

To this day, Morris feels that getting Landry to agree to allow FCA to use his name in creating the Tom Landry Associates program was the most important contribution he ever made.

Over the last 20-plus years, the Tom Landry Associates have contributed in excess of $166 million to FCA. There were 545 people who qualified as Tom Landry Associates in 2001-02, an all-time high, surpassed again in 2002-03 with 579. There have been 1,725 different Tom Landry Associates since 1981.

There have been 19 people who have given more than $1 million in their lifetimes, 24 have given between $500,000 and $1 million, 80 have given between $250,000 and $500,000, and 318 have given between $100,000 and $250,000.

You'd have to say that Ron Morris was right. ✝

To this day, Ron Morris (above) credits Tom Landry lending his name to the program for the success it has attained.

Specialized Diversity

The roots of FCA's sport-specific ministry can be traced back 26 years. In 1977, FCA regional director and retired Naval Officer Bill Lewis took his love of, and skill in, golf to the next level by founding the FCA National Golf Ministry.

"I approached (FCA President) John Erickson about moving into a full-time golf ministry, and he said we had no funding for the program," Lewis recalled. "He also told me that if I wanted to start it and raise the funds, I was on my own. That's all the go-ahead I needed."

He met with John Montgomery, the president of Executive Sports, Inc., which ran golf tournaments for the PGA Tour. Lewis shared his idea for a full-time ministry just for golfers, and Montgomery told him the golfing world needed it.

Montgomery also was key in introducing Lewis to Barbara Nicklaus, the wife of golf legend Jack Nicklaus. Lewis walked a round of a tournament with her in Ponte Vedra Beach, Fla., and shared his ideas of ministry.

"I approached John and Barbara and asked if they would raise $100,000 for the golf ministry." Lewis recalled. They came up with the idea for the first FCA International Pro-Am, which continues today. One of the first avenues of ministry was a junior golf camp at Pine Needles Resort, owned by FCA benefactor Peggy Kirk Bell. This past summer, more than 500 young people attended 19 FCA Golf Camps around the country.

Following Bill Lewis was another retired naval officer, Chaplain and Captain John Dolaghan. Under Dolaghan's leadership, FCA Golf added ministry to the pros on what is now called the Nationwide Tour, and to young golfers through "Breakfast with the Pros" outreach events.

Current FCA Golf Executive Director, Dean Bouzeos, a 19-year FCA staff member, has expanded ministry efforts by coordinating the FCA National Golf Scramble, a 140-tournament, 35-state event that shares Christ and raises funds for local FCA offices. In addition, the FCA Golf Ministry is seeking to expand its influence with golf coaches, club professionals and mini-tour pros. ⇨

Peggy Kirk Bell

FCA Golf has been going strong for more than 25 years. From Bill Lewis (top) to John Dolaghan to Dean Bouzeos (right in lower left photo), strong leadership has been the key.

Women's golf pioneer Peggy Kirk Bell is a big bene-factor of FCA Golf. Every year, she hosts a retreat for FCA supporters that includes golf at her legendary Pine Needles Lodge and Golf Club in Pine Needles, N.C.

The FCA Lacrosse Ministry started with a Camp in the summer of 1988, with eight campers. Former FCA Trustee Frank Kelly, who has been integral to the birth and success of the Lacrosse Ministry, was there and laughs about the challenges of conducting scrimmages with 40 percent of the players needed for a full game.

"We got awfully tired of three-on-three and four-on-four that summer," Kelly said. That fall at the national lacrosse coaches convention, FCA hosted its first breakfast. "We didn't even have a room," Kelly said. "They put us in the corner of the lobby. But God used that first outreach to plant a seed. It has grown from 20 coaches to more than 300 who attend each year."

A little more than two years later, at the 1991 Lacrosse Camp

at Gettysburg College, Kelly and four other coaches talked about the best way to make an impact in the sport. They decided to field a team in the prestigious Vail Shootout, something that looked bleak until right before it happened.

But FCA not only fielded a team to compete against the best teams in the country, it advanced all the way to the championship game. Returning from that tournament, they made the decision to start the lacrosse ministry as a separate entity. An Adult Chapter was started, which eventually led into the separate ministry.

FCA's Lacrosse Ministry Director, Sean McNamara, is a product of the ministry. At a Camp in 1992, as a high school sophomore, McNamara accepted Christ as his Savior. He played on the FCA team in future Vail Shootouts and eventually came on staff in 1999.

Today, the ministry has 4,000 members and three full-time staff. More than 300 kids attend FCA Lacrosse Camps each summer and 16 college lacrosse teams have team Bible studies sponsored by FCA Lacrosse.

In 2003, FCA added baseball to the list of sports-specific ministries, with others likely to appear in ⇨

FELLOWSHIP OF CHRISTIAN ATHLETES
B A S E B A L L

Much like the golf ministry, FCA Lacrosse is about teaching the sport and the Good News of Christ to the next generation. Baseball is next in line in this model.

the near future. Mike Lusardi, a 23-year veteran of Athletes In Action, joined FCA staff to head the baseball ministry.

"FCA gave me a great opportunity to do what I always wanted to do— build a national baseball ministry," Lusardi said. "FCA provides the best vehicle.

"We'll work with professional baseball players, utilizing the contacts I have and those in FCA. Outreach is the thrust. We want to share Christ using the platform of baseball. We'll also minister to the ballplayers and coaches."

The ministry of FCA is still for athletes and coaches and all whom they influence. There doesn't need to be a focus on a specific sport in order to be successful. But through the efforts of Lewis and others like him, FCA has learned that the sport-specific approach can work as well. ✝

Over the Top

Bill Burnett made a name for himself in Arkansas football history by leaping over the defensive line in short-yardage situations. When he landed on the other side, he usually carried a first down, or better yet, a touchdown. He did the latter well enough that he held the NCAA career record for touchdowns for nearly two decades.

Burnett went around, through and mostly over defenses to score 49 touchdowns in his three-year varsity career (he missed five games with an injury during his senior year) that ended in 1970. It took Indiana's Anthony Thompson four years to break the record. (He had 43 after three years, 68 total.) The next highest total in Arkansas' storied history is 39 (James Rouse, 1985-89).

Burnett also set an NCAA record for scoring touchdowns in 23 consecutive games. That record held until late in the 2002 season when Virginia Tech's Lee Suggs scored in his 24th straight.

"He wasn't particularly fast," said Rick Schaeffer, the director of development for the Northwest Arkansas FCA and the sports information director for Arkansas from 1976-2000. "He was slippery. He was a tough guy to bring down, especially when he went airborne."

Burnett was part of the Arkansas team that played in the Southwest Conference's version of the "greatest college football game ever played," when No. 1-ranked Texas beat No. 2-ranked Arkansas 15-14 on a last-minute touchdown in 1969.

When his playing career was finished, Burnett took FCA "over the top" in Arkansas, becoming the first full-time field staff member paid by the local area in FCA history. H.D. McCarty, pastor of University Baptist Church in Fayetteville, Ark., helped Burnett

get his financial footing. From there, it was onward and upward.

Burnett developed the first leadership board and held the first fundraising telethon, with guests that included major league baseball players Brooks Robinson and Don Kessinger, and Arkansas' own Frank Broyles. He also started the first FCA Camp in the state of Arkansas.

When current Arkansas football coach Houston Nutt was a senior at Little Rock Central High School, Burnett used to come by the high school once a week after practice to lead a Bible study. Burnett was an official "legend" in the state, so the young Nutt took notice.

Recently, Nutt told Schaeffer that Burnett was his "role model." "To have someone of Bill Burnett's stature take an interest in us made a big impression on me," Nutt said.

Today, Nutt is a supporter of FCA in the area, both with his words and his time. FCA can trace that support to Burnett's influence.

Burnett stayed on staff until 1980. He still serves on the state board and speaks to Camps and Huddles around the state whenever asked to do so.

"I never left FCA," Burnett says. "I was always involved on a volunteer basis. That's because of the impact I've seen it have—not only in my life but in countless other lives."

Burnett's generosity also has blessed FCA in the state to the point where Arkansas FCA is one of the most successful state organizations in the ministry.

"He's still extremely influential in development for FCA in the entire state of Arkansas," Schaeffer said. "Between Coach Broyles and him, FCA couldn't have a better pair of ambassadors anywhere in the country."✝

Bill Burnett continues to make an impact in Arkansas.

1972

Swimmer Mark Spitz wins seven gold medals at Olympics in Munich.

Miami Dolphins complete perfect 17-0 season.

Political operatives break in to the Democratic Party headquarters in the Watergate building in Washington, D.C.

Television show *M*A*S*H* debuts.

A Mercedes 250 costs $7,800. A Dodge Duster costs $1,993.

1973

| Congress passes Title IX, requiring equal opportunity for females in athletics. | Billie Jean King defeats Bobby Riggs in tennis' "Battle of the Sexes." | A cease-fire is declared in the Vietnam War. U.S. combat troops come home. | Vice-President Spiro Agnew resigns. Congressman Gerald Ford is appointed Vice President. | Pet rocks are a fad. |

No Mulligan Needed

Mallory Code takes 40 pills a day when she is healthy, 60 when she is sick. She has had 13 sinus surgeries, so far. And every three days, she moves the insulin pump in her stomach from one side to the other. She also hits a mean drive down the fairway.

Diagnosed with four diseases by the time she was 15—cystic fibrosis, asthma, sinusitis and diabetes—Code has not allowed injury or illness to keep her from becoming one of golf's finest up-and-comers. Currently enjoying a full athletic scholarship to the University of Florida, Code recognizes that her game is different from that of her peers.

"I take care of what I need to between shots," says Code, a regular speaker at FCA events. "It doesn't affect my game when I'm on the course. However, overall it does affect my game, because I occasionally have to take time off for IV's or surgery."

But this way of life has become as normal to Code as swinging a golf club.

"I've been going out to the golf course for as long as I can remember," says Code, who followed her two older siblings onto the American Junior Golf Association (AJGA) tour when she was 13. Her first tour victory came in April of 2000 in Columbia Lakes, Texas, after shooting rounds of 73 and 75 to win by one stroke.

But as great an accomplishment as a first tour victory was, the second brought Code even more respect. At the July 2000, AJGA Rolex Tournament of Champions in El Dorado Hills, Calif., Code shot rounds of 70, 73, 72 and 73 to win by two strokes—while wearing a heart monitor.

This ability to overcome obstacles stems from Code's unwavering faith in Christ. Growing up in a Christian home, she was exposed to the Bible at an early age.

"When my mom would tuck me in bed, she would ask me if I had asked Jesus into my heart," she says. "I would tell her 'yes' because I really wasn't sure, and that sounded like the better side to err on. But when I really asked myself if I had, I realized I hadn't. So I accepted the Lord one night while lying in bed."

As her faith has grown, the Lord has given Code a platform from which to share her source of strength. She has spoken at numerous fund-raisers for the Cystic Fibrosis Foundation and the Children's Miracle Network, and even has appeared at the Boomer Esiason Foundation's Booming Celebration for Cystic Fibrosis.

No matter where or when she speaks, Code keeps one central theme. "I always try to give God as much credit as possible and stress how grateful I am for everything He has done." ✝

Mallory Code improved her golf skills at FCA Golf Camp and her leadership skills at FCA Leadership Camp.

"Then he said to them all:
'If anyone would come after me, he
must deny himself and take up his
cross daily and follow me.'"

—Luke 9:23

Adventure

Hail to the Chiefs

What do these men have in common?

- A college basketball manager and later a college coach;

- A teacher and high school football coach;

- A college football star and insurance executive;

- A college basketball coach and NBA executive;

- A college football coach and Air Force General;

- A college football player and coach, sandwiched around being a Marine.

These describe the six men who have been Executive Director or President of the Fellowship of Christian Athletes during its first 50 years of ministry. All brought strong convictions about their faith in Jesus Christ, a heart for athletes and coaches, and a passion for FCA and its unique ministry in a sports-crazed society. All were laymen and none had a theology degree.

Their leadership qualities, strengths, talents and abilities have been used by God in a timely fashion.

Each was chosen and ordained by God for his "moment in time" to serve when his gifts for leadership were most needed by FCA. Significant developments took place in each one's tenure.

DON McCLANEN: God planted the idea for FCA into the heart of a humble man named Don McClanen. He was a basketball manager for legendary coach Henry Iba at Oklahoma A&M.

The founding father of FCA was born in Trenton, N.J. He grew up in Morrisville, Pa. A World War II Navy veteran, he enrolled at Oklahoma A&M after his discharge. As a 22-year-old sophomore in 1947, McClanen gave a speech entitled, "Making My Vocation Christian."

The idea of FCA was planted in his heart. In 1954, after seven years of prayer, patience and determined zeal, the dream came true and FCA was chartered. He left his basketball coaching job at Eastern Oklahoma State University and became Executive Director of the new ministry. ⇨

Dal Shealy (above), FCA's sixth President, has been involved in football as a player, coach and administrator for more than 50 years.

McClanen

Stoddard

Jeffrey

Erickson

Abel

Shealy

He served for eight years from 1954-62. A man of vision, McClanen founded two other ministries called Washington Lift and Ministry of Money. He and his wife, Gloria, live in Germantown, Md.

BOB STODDARD: After compiling a 43-4-2 record with 33 consecutive wins as head football coach at Carmel (N.Y.) High School, Stoddard joined the FCA staff in Kansas City on June 15, 1960. Stoddard teamed with McClanen and Gary Demarest and came on staff two months before FCA staged two national Camps in one year for the first time.

Possessed with a loving and enthusiastic spirit, Stoddard became Executive Director in the summer of 1962 after McClanen resigned. While traveling in New York for FCA, he died of a coronary occlusion in a New York City hospital January 24, 1963, hours after a racquetball game. He was 38. His wife, Shirley, directed Camp registration for FCA for 26 years and still lives in Kansas City.

JAMES JEFFREY: As Executive Director of FCA from 1963-71, "Jeff" was known as "Mr. FCA." He came from a highly successful insurance business in Texas and was well known as an All-Southwest Conference halfback at Baylor University. His high energy and radiant spirit captivated audiences across America as a speaker, magician and juggler. From 1956-72, he attended every FCA summer Camp.

Early growth of high school and college Huddles and Adult Chapters came during Jeffrey's tenure. Many outstanding men were added to the staff across America, and Camps flourished. He resigned in February 1972 and remained in Kansas City as a community servant for many Christian and charitable causes. Jeffrey died on May 30, 1991, at age 61, after a long battle with cancer.

JOHN ERICKSON: Holding the distinction of serving the longest tenure as FCA President from 1972-88, Erickson provided outstanding, innovative leadership. He restructured the Board of Trustees; led in the National Conference Center development in Indiana; established FCA's women's ministry, junior high and inner-city programs; saw the Coaches Camps take off

and spearheaded the construction of the National Headquarters building, which was dedicated in May 1979 during FCA's 25th anniversary.

Erickson was a standout athlete at Beloit College (Wis.), head basketball coach at the University of Wisconsin (1958-68) and served as Vice President and General Manager of the expansion Milwaukee Bucks. After FCA, he became assistant commissioner of the Big Eight Conference. He and his wife, Polly, still are active with FCA and live in Kansas City.

DICK ABEL: The fifth President of FCA had been Director of Public Affairs for the United States Air Force as a Brigadier General. He greeted the first group of 120 POWs released at the end of the Vietnam War. On February 1, 1988, he began a vigorous FCA presidency adding new staff leadership positions. Huddles increased 100 percent and Leadership Camps doubled.

Much expansion and growth through modern technology had incredible results during Abel's tenure. A native of Cleveland, Abel played football at the University of Detroit and later coached football at the Air Force Academy, where he became a Christian at an FCA meeting. He resigned in February 1992 and became the National Director of Military Ministry for Campus Crusade for Christ. He and his wife, Ann, live in Newport News, Va.

DAL SHEALY: Shealy came to FCA in January 1989 as Executive Vice President in charge of field staff and ministry programs from the University of Richmond, where as head football coach he took the Spiders to the NCAA I-AA playoffs twice in nine years. He has been involved in organized football and college sports for more than 50 years as player, coach and motivator of young athletes.

Shealy first played football at Batesburg-Leesville High School in South Carolina and continued playing at Carson-Newman College. He then entered military service and played with the Quantico Marines, which were National Service Champions. He accepted his first coaching position at Laurens (S.C.) High School in football and track.⇨

John Erickson helped FCA gain much visibility, including throwing out the first pitch of Game 3 of the 1980 World Series.

1974

| Hank Aaron hits 715th home run. | A national speed limit of 55 miles-per-hour is imposed. | President Richard Nixon resigns. | Evil Knievel fails in his attempt to jump the Snake River Canyon in his jet-propelled craft. | Philippe Petit walks along a 1-inch-wide wire strung between the towers of the World Trade Center in New York. |

Shealy then served as head coach at Mars-Hill College and Carson-Newman. He later served on the staffs at Baylor, Tennessee, Auburn and Iowa State as assistant head coach and/or offensive coordinator. He went to Richmond in 1980 to reinstate the football program.

Shealy was inducted into the Carson-Newman Hall of Fame in 1986 and was selected to the Carson-Newman College Team of the Century in 1994. He received the 2002 award for "Outstanding Contribution to Amateur Football" from the National Football Foundation/College Hall of Fame.

Late in 2003, he received the Order of the Silver Crescent from the state of South Carolina for exemplary contributions to the Palmetto State. It is the highest award given to a South Carolina native.

Shealy was introduced to FCA at a coaches breakfast in the mid-1960s in Chicago "because it was free, and I was a young coach on a shoestring budget." Later, at an FCA Camp at Black Mountain, N.C., he recommitted his life to Christ. Shealy led FCA Huddles at the schools where he coached and served on local and state boards.

As President/CEO, he has led FCA through record growth in Huddles, participating student-athletes and coaches, Camps, staff, and revenue. During Shealy's tenure, FCA has grown from 190 staff members to more than 600, the National Office was remodeled and then expanded to more than double the size, and the National Conference Center was remodeled.

Following the 2000 Olympics in Sydney, Australia, Shealy was one of the presenters at a conference of 350 sports-ministry leaders from 80 countries.

He led the restructuring and realignment of the ministry, and the introduction of FCA's global ministry, where FCA resources and/or personnel are making an impact in 80 different countries. He spearheaded the growth and development of the *One Way 2 Play-Drug Free!* program, which embodies the elements of faith, commitment and accountability. He also was behind the launch of two other sport-specific ministries—lacrosse and baseball—to go along with the growing golf ministry.

Most importantly, he has been a leader of impeccable character, who inspires those who work with him to give their best to serve an "Audience of One." ✝

1975

| Carlton Fisk of the Boston Red Sox hits dramatic home run in Game 6 of World Series. | *Jaws* debuts. | *Saturday Night Live* premiers. | Fred Lynn of the Boston Red Sox becomes first player to win AL Rookie of the Year and MVP Awards in the same year. | Jimmy Hoffa disappears. |

Training For
a Spiritual Battle

Heather Mercer was big news during the summer of 2001. What was less-known by the watching nation was the role that FCA played in her preparation for the ordeal she endured.

Mercer was one of eight missionaries working for Shelter Now International who were arrested by Taliban officials in August 2001 for sharing their faith with Afghan nationals. The nationals were required by law to follow the teachings of Islam.

After a daring rescue by the U.S. Military, with help from the local residents, the group was reunited with family and friends, plus a nation that had been praying for them. They visited the White House, where President George W. Bush told them he had been praying for them. They did not shy away from telling people that their strength came from Jesus Christ.

"It's clear in the New Testament over and over again that God uses suffering and trials to change people," Mercer said. "This whole experience, though at times it was a big struggle, has been the biggest privilege of my life, because God has used the trials to really show me who He is, that He is real and He is near, that I can trust Him no matter what, and that He answers prayer."

During their three-and-a-half-month ordeal, people across the United States and the world were praying for their release, a miracle that didn't appear likely in the days and weeks following the terrorist attacks on September 11, 2001.

But for Mercer, the miracle was that God loved her enough to send His Son for her. She was just following through on a promise she made to Him at an FCA meeting.

She first got involved in FCA when she was a freshman in high school, before she was a Christian. She had

been going through a tumultuous time in her life, and friends at school invited her to start attending FCA meetings.

"My track coach and my friends had a huge influence on me," she said. "They loved me and lived out Jesus in front of me. FCA was the first place I was discipled and learned how to follow Jesus in a personal way."

She accepted Jesus into her life at an FCA rally. "I went up and just started bawling," she said. "I felt a real change in my heart. I knew that something was different. I couldn't explain it at the time, but that was when Jesus got ahold of my heart.

"I learned that if God changed me, the love of God had to come back out. I couldn't hide it inside. There were so many other people like me who just had to hear about His love."

Mercer jumped head-first into FCA. She attended the Madison (Va.) Huddle with renewed enthusiasm, eventually becoming one of the officers. She attended Bible studies at her church and at school to learn more about Christ.

Mercer also attended two FCA Camps. "FCA provided a great vehicle as an athlete to be able to invite people to a safe place where they could hear about Jesus," she said. "It was a place where they could connect with people and build relationships, and not feel intimidated."

After high school, she went to Baylor University in Waco, Texas. She started attending Antioch Community Church, where she caught the vision of serving God in another country.

"It was during my sophomore year in college that God made it clear that I was supposed to spend my life overseas in some kind of missions work," she said. "During my time in college, I asked God to send me to a place that no one else wanted to go and minister. One of those places was Afghanistan. ⇨

"FCA provided a great vehicle as an athlete to be able to invite people to a safe place where they could hear about Jesus."

As a high school student, Heather Mercer (highlighted) had no idea of the ordeal she would endure, but her FCA training definitely prepared her.

"After my junior year, I went with some friends to visit Afghanistan to see if it was a place I could live. When I went, I fell in love with the people. I remember that when I got on the plane to go home, I started crying because I knew that was the place I was supposed to go."

She went back to Afghanistan as a full-time missionary after graduation. After building a relationship with a family whose children begged on the streets all day, she and her fellow missionaries went to the family's house to share about Jesus. As they left the house that day, the Taliban guards were waiting to arrest them.

They spent the next three and a half months being moved from one prison to another. Some were desolate and depressing. The others were far worse. The conditions were inhumane, and the constant threat of torture or execution sometimes challenged Mercer and her team. But their faith kept them focused on God.

"Right at the beginning, we had a sense that it was God who allowed us to be in prison. It was not the Taliban who kept us there. It was God, because He had a greater purpose in mind for us. Now, we've seen more evidence of what that purpose is. He used our experience to change us, change the nation and even change the world."

"I dealt with fear like never before," she said. "I knew these guys could do whatever they wanted. I remembered that I was willing when I came here, but I never had to look death in the face and say I was ready or willing to die. I fought with God. I fought with Him hard, and I lost. I asked God if He is real and who He says He is. Does He really answer prayers and fulfill His promises? It didn't look like it right then.

"It wasn't until I finally said, 'Jesus, You have my life. It all belongs to You. I told You I would come here and serve You, no matter what the cost. And now You're taking me at my word. It's all about You. If I live, I live for You. If I die, I die for You. Whatever will advance Your Name the most, I'll do it."

It ended as suddenly as it began. The Taliban soldiers guarding the group were forced to leave, so they put their prisoners in a steel shipping container and scattered. The prisoners were rescued later that day.

"There were times when we had a glimpse into Heaven," Mercer said, reflecting on the ordeal. "We realized that we were blessed to be in prison and to be persecuted for the Name of Jesus. Jesus was persecuted for the message He shared. To get to walk a similar road that Jesus walked is the greatest honor of my life."✝

Once a week before school, Mercer would meet Huddle leader Cynthia Rahal (center, above) and fellow student Mindi Hardison to study the Word. Upon her return, she and Dayna Curry had another impressive meeting.

Calling the Right Plays

College quarterbacks are always at the center of attention.

All eyes are on the quarterback before the football is snapped. He's the leader on the field. He is a skilled athlete and many times a star, even the most valuable player. He is the envy of wannabe players. His performance is often the key to victory.

Through the years, dozens of college quarterbacks have used their platform and influence in FCA. Beginning in the early 1960s with college FCA campus fellowships, players such as Steve Sloan (Alabama), Roger Staubach and Bruce Bickel (Navy), Pat Screen (LSU), Bob Timberlake (Michigan), Sam Wyche (Furman) and Jimmy Sidle (Auburn) were not ashamed to express their faith in Jesus Christ.

Sloan spoke at the Billy Graham Crusade in Greenville, S.C. his senior year in 1966 and soon published a book, *Calling Life's Signals*, about his young life. Staubach became one of FCA's finest ambassadors with the Dallas Cowboys, and Bickel was a longtime FCA staff member.

The 60s also saw Rex Kern (Ohio State) as a strong believer and active FCA participant, besides leading his team to the Rose Bowl. Kern started the FCA breakfast on the Saturday morning prior to the Ohio State spring game. That breakfast just celebrated its 35th anniversary. Bob Anderson (Colorado) was a 1969 All-American quarterback and was selected co-collegiate FCA Athlete of the Year.

In the 1970s, Jack Mildren (Oklahoma), James Street (Texas) and Bill Montgomery (Arkansas) were three of the nation's top quarterbacks. All three participated in the Dallas Weekend of Champions in 1971. Jeff Hollenbach (Illinois), Scott Hall (Wheaton), Steadman Shealy (Alabama), Rocky Felker (Mississippi State), Maurie Daigneau (Northwestern), Ray Goff (Georgia), David Lee (Vanderbilt), Cam Cameron (Indiana), Johnny Evans (North Carolina State) and Tommy Nelson (North Texas State) were outspoken about their faith through FCA.

Lee is on the Dallas Cowboys coaching staff. Cameron was recipient of the Bob Stoddard Award given to ⇨

Jay Barker (above) and Todd Blackledge (right) are just two of the many college quarterbacks who have led their school's Huddles.

the nation's most outstanding FCA high school athlete and later became head coach at Indiana. Nelson has become a prominent pastor and national speaker from the Denton (Texas) Bible Church. Evans has served many years on the FCA staff in North Carolina (see page 146).

Neal, John and Jay Jeffrey, sons of former FCA Executive Director James Jeffrey, were role models as Christian athletes. Neal and Jay led Baylor to two Cotton Bowl appearances and John performed well as a Bears tight end. Neal also was the FCA National Player of the Year after his senior year.

J.C. Watts led strong Oklahoma teams in the late 70s and went on to be a United States Congressman. He was inducted into FCA's Hall of Champions in 1997.

In the 1980s Bobby Hebert became a Christian through the Northwestern St. (La.) University FCA Huddle and spent many years with the New Orleans Saints. Neil Lomax (Portland State) was a strong FCA leader and a Christian spokesman while with the St. Louis Cardinals. Mike Shula (Alabama), Jeff Hostetler (West Virginia), Steve Pelluer (Washington), Marty Louthan (Air Force), Walter Lewis (Alabama) and Kent Kiefer (Missouri) were active FCA'ers, as was Todd Blackledge (Penn State), who has become a popular ⇨

college football broadcaster. Darin Slack (South Florida) later became the Central Florida FCA representative.

More outstanding young men came through the FCA quarterback ranks in the 1990s. Charlie Ward (Florida State) and Danny Wuerffel (Florida) were Heisman Trophy winners in 1993 and 1997 respectfully. "FCA gave me an avenue to hear the Word," Ward said. "It was kind of like going to church in the middle of the week."

Wuerffel made a strong statement when he opted not to accept a spot on the *Playboy* All-American team.

Alabama All-American Jay Barker led the Crimson Tide to a national championship in 1992 but was known best by his statement: "I've never tasted alcohol, nor taken drugs and I'm a virgin." Trent Dilfer (Fresno State) made a decision to follow Christ totally at a 1992 FCA Camp. He has since become a Super Bowl-winning quarterback (see page 144).

Danny Kanell (Florida State), Blane Morgan (Air Force), Patrick Nix (Auburn) and Shaun King (Tulane) also were active in FCA.

Nebraska's Tommie Frazier and Brook Berringer led the Cornhuskers to national championships in 1994 and 1995. A book followed on Frazier entitled *Touchdown Tommie*. On April 18, 1996, late in his senior year, Berringer died in a plane crash the day he was to speak at an FCA Banquet in Lincoln (see page 46). His story also is chronicled in a book, *One Final Pass*. Scott Frost succeeded them as FCA leader.

As the year 2000 began, Major Applewhite (Texas) was a refreshing young man who exemplified humility as a star and gave FCA and the Lord his all. Josh Heupel led Oklahoma to the national title in 2000 and lifted Christ in his play. Brian Madden (Navy) was a fine FCA leader at the Academy. Chris Rix (Florida State) warns young people against alcohol, drugs and sexual immorality and encourages their involvement in church and FCA.

Spiritual obedience among these and countless other college quarterbacks has born much fruit touching millions of lives through FCA.

"Let your light shine before men that they may see your good deeds and praise your Father in Heaven." —(Matthew 5:16)✝

The list includes Mike Shula (top left), Neal Jeffrey (top right) and Brian Madden (right).

Nadia Comaneci becomes first gymnast to earn a perfect "10" in Olympic competition.

The United States of America celebrates its Bicentennial.

Steve Jobs and Steve Wozniak invent the Apple I computer, the first true "personal computer."

Rocky wins Best Picture Oscar.

The spacecraft Viking I lands on Mars and sends back photographs of its surface.

1977

Egyptian president Anwar Sadat visits Jerusalem. Israel's prime minister Menachem Begin visits Egypt.

Reggie Jackson hits three World Series home runs on three pitches, confirming the nickname "Mr. October."

Elvis Presley dies at age 42.

The "Johnstown (Pa.) Flood" occurs when 12" of rain falls in seven hours.

Star Wars is a box office blockbuster hit.

A Man of His Word

Branch Rickey is known in baseball circles as "the Father of Modern Day Baseball." He's known in FCA circles as one of the architects of the movement that is celebrating its 50th anniversary.

But if we could be so presumptuous, in God's eyes, there is one description that stands above the rest—a man of his word.

When Rickey wanted to make baseball a career at the turn of the 20th century, he encountered resistance from his parents. Baseball players were hardly the role models they are today—quite the opposite.

So he made a deal with his mother. If she allowed him to play baseball, he promised not to go to games on Sundays. This showed how badly he wanted to pursue this venture, and showed his parents that the values they had instilled in him, including honoring the Sabbath, were still elements of his life.

Rickey played major league baseball for four seasons. He managed for 10 seasons, and he was a baseball executive for the remainder of his life, which lasted another 45 years. Long after his parents were gone, he still stayed away from the ballpark on Sundays.

"What is so significant to me about that was that he always explained that primarily he had made a promise to his mother," said Branch B. Rickey, the grandson of the baseball legend. "Even when he was a manager, he always had somebody designated as his 'Sunday manager.'

"For several decades after his mother had passed away, he kept that promise, because it was a promise he made. I think it is a very powerful example of how much he believed in choosing your options and standing by your word."

He earned the "Father of Modern Day Baseball" tag for some of his innovations that seem commonplace today. He thought up the idea of farm systems, minor league teams that train players for future

✠

"Of all the men I met in baseball, Mr. Rickey was the finest, in a class by himself."
—Jackie Robinson

✠

major league service. He was the first executive to hold "Ladies Days" at the stadium to attract female fans, and the "Knothole Gang" to attract young fans. His teams were the first to travel by plane instead of train.

In 1947, he signed African-American Jackie Robinson with the idea of integrating Major League Baseball after decades of being "a white man's game."

"It isn't right to say I broke the color line," Robinson would say later. "Mr. Rickey did. I played ball. Mr. Rickey made it possible for me to play. Of all the men I met in baseball, Mr. Rickey was the finest, in a class by himself."

Robinson was not the logical choice. He was not the most talented man in the Negro Leagues. He also was a bit of a hot-head.

"(Robinson) was not an ideal man for the job," Rickey told the audience at the first FCA Camp ⇨

Rickey's decision to sign Robinson to a Major League contract changed the face of baseball forever.

in 1956. "He was resentful of criticism, quickly retaliating to insults by nature. He had a sense of tremendous injustice that any should discriminate against him because of different pigmentation of skin."

But Rickey reminded the young ballplayer that Jesus responded to insults and criticisms that were far more unfair than what Robinson had to endure. It made a difference that resulted in Robinson's Hall of Fame career.

"(Robinson's Christian faith) was the core of my grandfather's regard for Jackie," the younger Rickey said. "My grandfather's greatest skill was his ability

to assess those around him, to measure them, to evaluate them.

"I never saw him make an evaluation of a person's religious commitment by what the person said. He was interested in whether the person was true to his beliefs."

So when Don McClanen approached him about supporting a new idea he had for a ministry based on athletes sharing their faith, Rickey measured McClanen's idea with his commitment and devotion. The result was summarized in Rickey's speech at the first FCA Camp. ⇨

Rickey was a popular banquet speaker
in the early days of FCA.

"This Fellowship of Christian Athletes is not a namby-pamby thing; it is a courageous organization. It is not a physical conditioning process; it is a cooperative grouping of athletes to embrace and have others embrace Jesus as the Christ, the measure of divinity through which we come to find and know God. It is an effort that challenges our best intelligence and all our emotions. We must proceed to the task with conviction, with contriteness and with courage, even to the point of ardor.

"I don't think I've ever been faced with a situation that seemed to be so pregnant with potential as the immediate possibilities of a great crowd of young men coming to feel the presence of God and the duty of service to the King of kings.

"The potential is almost beyond conception."

Rickey continued to support the ministry for the next nine years, until his death in 1965. He supported it financially, and with his time and his words. That, of course, was no surprise.

After all, he gave his word. ✞

A Cut Above

The Fellowship of Christian Athletes Hall of Champions is a body of Teammates in Christ, elected by a committee to honor those who have demonstrated a consistent commitment to, and support of, FCA's purpose:

"To present to athletes and coaches, and all whom they influence, the challenge and adventure of receiving Jesus Christ as their personal Savior and Lord, serving Him in their relationships and in the fellowship of the church."

The criteria for nomination includes, but is not limited to, those whose life has demonstrated:

- A personal belief in and commitment to Jesus Christ as their Savior and Lord;

- A commitment to active participation in the ministry of FCA;

- A commitment to further FCA's purpose;

- An involvement in day-to-day FCA activities, Camps, Huddles, special events and other programs;

- A lengthy period of consistent service (minimum of 10 years).

Teaff

Yow

Towler

Osborne

FCA HALL OF CHAMPIONS

Class of 1991

Tom Landry	Football Coach
Archie Griffin	Heisman Trophy Winner
Steve Owens	Heisman Trophy Winner
Roger Staubach	Heisman Trophy Winner
James N. Jeffrey	FCA Executive Director
Dick Lane	Volunteer
Dan Stavely	Football Coach

Class of 1992

Paul Anderson	U.S. Olympian
Kay Yow	Basketball Coach
Jerry Kindall	Baseball Coach
Betsy King	LPGA Golfer

Class of 1994

Peggy Kirk Bell	LPGA Golfer
Nick Hyder	High School Coach
Don McClanen	FCA Founder and Executive Director

Class of 1995

Steve Largent	Congressman and Football Player
Branch Rickey	Baseball Executive

Class of 1997

J.C. Watts	Congressman and Football Player
John Wooden	Basketball Coach
Raymond Berry	Football Coach

Class of 1998

Bunny Martin	Volunteer
Bobby Richardson	Baseball Player
Dick Schultz	Volunteer
Grant Teaff	Football Coach
Harry J. Lloyd	Volunteer

Class of 1999

Tonya Crevier	Basketball Handler
"Deacon" Dan Towler	Football Player
Don Shinnick	Football Player

Class of 2000

Tony Dungy	Football Coach
Faye O'Dell	Football Coach
Captain Bill Lewis	FCA Golf Ministry Founder

Class of 2001

Jane Albright	Basketball Coach
Bobby Bowden	Football Coach
John Lotz	College Administrator
Freddy Mitchell	Volunteer
Tom Osborne	Football Coach

Class of 2002

Carl Erskine	Baseball Player
John Erickson	FCA President
Danny Lotz	Basketball Player
R.V. Brown	Football Player
Morley Fraser	Athletics Director

Class of 2003

Dr. O.K. Bailey	Volunteer
Ray Hildebrand	Former Staff/Volunteer
Mike Singletary	Football Player
Jim Myers	Football Coach
Joan Cronan	Athletics Director

Faithful Leadership

Some of the nation's most respected and admired men and women have served on the Fellowship of Christian Athletes Board of Trustees during the past half-century.

Paramount to a highly visible Christian movement are leaders and successful people who pooled their decision-making skills to move the organization in the right direction, to keep it Christ-centered and controlled with integrity and character.

Over the past 50 years, FCA has experienced financial struggles, had tough personnel decisions, sought to launch new programs and investigated countless other ventures that demanded wise decisions. National—and eventually international—in scope, it required people from the four corners of the nation and the world to share their expertise, experience, wisdom and vision. Thus, decisions made at hundreds of board meetings have moved the Fellowship of Christian Athletes to the dynamic national ministry it is today.

Founder Don McClanen was blessed with highly respected men such as Dr. Louis Evans, pastor of the First Presbyterian Church of Hollywood, Calif. Roe Johnston, a Navy All-American football player and Presbyterian minister also, was the first Board of Directors Chairman.

As FCA became a reality, there were three principal governing bodies: the Board of Directors, the Advisory Committee and the Honorary Trustees. Branch Rickey headed up the 10-man Honorary Trustees. The Advisory Committee was made up of 28 highly revered athletes, coaches and clergymen.

Fifteen men served on the Board of Directors in its initial years. Board meetings were held in conjunction with the Estes Park, Colo., FCA Camp. The first five Board Chairmen were Johnston (1954-55), Evans (1956), "Biggie" Munn (1957-58), Otto Graham (1959-60) and Tad Wieman (1961). ⇨

The Board has grown in numbers through the years, but it always has included some of the biggest names in sports.

Board members during this era included Herb McCracken, Bob Taylor, Dick Harp, Donn Moomaw, Jim Stoner, Dick Armstrong, Ron Morris and H.B. "Bebe" Lee (1962 Chairman).

LSU football coach Paul Dietzel was Board Chairman in 1963-64, followed by Baylor football coach John Bridges in 1965-66. Duke football coach Bill Murray led the Board in 1967-68 and FCA charter member Donn Moomaw in 1969-70.

Arkansas football coach Frank Broyles was Board Chairman from 1971-73. At the height of his illustrious Dallas Cowboys reign, Coach Tom Landry served as Board Chairman from 1974-76. Fall Board meetings were held in Dallas, where he conducted Board business even during the football season.

FCA turned to four outstanding businessmen for the next 13 years to head the growing movement. They were Durand Holladay (1977-79), Tony Wauterlek (1980-83), Danny Danielson (1983-87) and Jim McCormick (1987-90).

While serving as Executive Director of the NCAA, Dick Schultz also served as Board Chairman from 1990-93.

Schultz was succeeded by Grant Teaff (1994-95), former Baylor football coach and currently the Executive Director of the American Football Coaches Association. Schultz and Teaff held two of the most important positions in amateur sports, yet devoted their time and energy to FCA at the same time. Their leadership brought the ultimate credibility to the ministry.

Chairmen who succeeded them were Gary Cuozzo (1995-99) and Nelson Price (1999-present).

Through the years FCA Board members were some of the nation's most prominent and respected figures. They included Bob Pettit, Alan Ameche, Dan Towler, Carl Erskine, Jack Robinson, Bill Wade, Lamar Hunt, Paul Anderson, Bowie Kuhn, Tom Osborne, Danny Lotz, Dean Smith, Len LeSourd, Peggy Kirk Bell, Kyle Rote, Jr., Madeline Manning Mims, Betsy King, Jake Gaither, Rex Kern, Sal Bando, Kay Yow, Terry Dissinger, Eddie Robinson and Marty Leonard. To list a few leaves out countless others who played roles just as significant.

John Erickson, former FCA President, reflecting on the value of the FCA Board said, "These men and women have brought integrity to the organization. They have been great people who have served well. They have met great challenges. I have observed tremendous commitment over the years, people who attended the meetings, gave sacrificially and made some tough decisions on many occasions. Their servanthood could never be measured in establishing where the Fellowship has soared today."✝

The Board of Trustees in 1982.

First indoor Super Bowl played (Dallas vs. Denver in Superdome in New Orleans).	The U.S. Supreme Court rules "reverse discrimination" is unconstitutional.	Pope Paul VI dies and Pope John Paul I is elected. When John Paul I dies a month later, Pope John Paul II is elected.	More than 900 Jim Jones Temple Cult Members die in murder-suicide in Guyana.	The Camp David peace accords between Egypt and Israel are signed.

1978

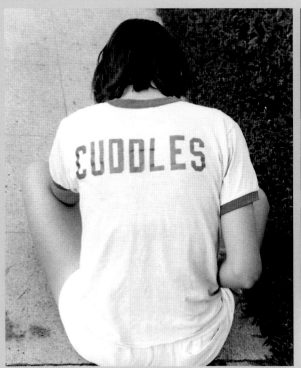

Changing Faces

The face of today's FCA barely resembles that of just three or four decades ago. Like many long-standing organizations, the Fellowship of Christian Athletes has had to grow and expand along with the changing world.

This expansion began in 1963. Highland Park Middle School had been pushing for three years to receive an official sanction for its FCA Huddle, but to no avail. Organization officials maintained that faith could not be taken seriously at such an early age.

But Huddle Coaches Al Dudley and Kellis White thought differently. They knew that their students were mature enough to have an authentic relationship with Christ, but it took some convincing before FCA would agree.

Through a series of timely contacts and events, White was able to spend a weekend with then-FCA President James Jeffrey, where White did his best to sell the idea of a junior high Huddle.

"I spent the weekend with him and just shared our situation and our vision," White said. "It wasn't long after that that we received our sanction. And I'm so appreciative of him, because he went to bat for us. He caught sight of our vision."

Eleven years after adopting Highland Park as the first junior high Huddle, FCA once again expanded its roster of participants.

With the 1973 introduction of Title IX—legislation requiring all Federally funded schools to provide equal opportunity for women in sports—the FCA Board of Trustees recognized a need to reach out to a growing population of female athletes.

Just two years later, FCA was ready to begin a new ministry. The first official action was to hold two national women's Camps at the National Conference Center in Indiana. In 1975, the first all-girls' Huddles (briefly referred to as "Cuddles") became official. And just one year later in 1976, FCA hired Cindy Smith as its first national women's director. ⇨

The addition of ministry to females and junior high students has kept FCA up-to-date with society.

"In my opinion, the women's ministry is not there for equal rights or women's lib. It's there out of our desire for young ladies to be presented with the Gospel and to grow in Christ," said former FCA staff member Debbie Wall-Larson in Wayne Atcheson's book *Impact for Christ*. "I know God has great things in store for FCA's ministry to women. When He is in control, we will be blessed beyond our highest expectations."

Today, more than 50 percent of Huddle leaders are females. Junior high Huddles account for more than 10 percent of all Huddles nationwide.

Barbara Shealy, wife of FCA President/CEO Dal Shealy, also has a ministry to coaches' wives. *Behind the Bench*, which started as a newsletter to 300 wives, now has a circulation of about 12,000. ✠

| USA Hockey upsets USSR in Olympic "Miracle On Ice." | Ted Turner launches CNN, the first all-news network. | The Soviet Union invades Afghanistan and the United States boycotts the Moscow Olympic Games. | Ronald Reagan is elected President. | The Rubik's Cube puzzles millions. |

| | Columbia, the first Space Shuttle, orbits Earth 36 times. | Major League Baseball season is "split" because of 59-day strike. | Ronald Reagan is shot in an assassination attempt. | Sandra Day O'Connor becomes first female Supreme Court Judge. | Prince Charles marries Lady Diana Spencer. |

1981

Peaceful Purpose

Where can you find football players, basketball players, soccer players and athletes from nearly every other sport, along with worship leaders, motivational speakers and youth workers? The FCA National Conference Center (NCC) in Marshall, Ind., has hosted these and many others in the 36 years since FCA originally purchased the land.

FCA purchased the land in 1967 from Don Lash, a former Olympian and world-record holder, through the generosity of the Lilly and Oberdorfer Foundations. Lash and his wife, Margaret, had purchased 60 acres of land and called it Camp Wapallo to make an impact on America's youth. The camp ministered to many, including several FCA Camps.

Charlie Miller became Director in 1971 when God threw the NCC into full swing. Miller was in charge of developing the first dorm, renovating the dining hall and laying out the 22-acre athletic fields and four-court basketball pavilion, which still are being used today.

The site was dedicated officially in June of 1975 with Dallas Cowboys coach Tom Landry, Indiana Governor Otis Bowen and FCA President John Erickson as part of the festivities. With that event came the unveiling of plans for the Kresge Chapel, which holds more than 250 people.

Since its completion in 1976, Kresge Chapel has seen thousands of people rededicate their lives to Christ and many come to know Him for the first time. Many times FCA campers return as Huddle Leaders or interns. Some even return as directors or coaches passing their experience to the next generation.

The NCC has kept the momentum going by adding facilities to increase its capacity from 150 to the current level of 254. In 1985, the NCC opened its doors year-round for FCA Camps and retreats, along with outside groups. Former Indiana University football coach Cam Cameron, who attended FCA Camps at the NCC, jumped at the chance to bring his team to the conference center for their annual training camp three years in a row.

Over the years, the NCC has seen many unique groups enjoy its facilities. The NCC now can offer challenging elements, including a 200-foot zip line, a rappelling wall, a climbing wall and other high-adventure opportunities. It also is equipped with athletic fields, nature trails, and most recently, an .8-mile motocross track.

The recent addition of the motocross track has enabled FCA to design a new Camp concept all its own. The idea was to reach the campers, their parents and even the instructors with the message of Jesus Christ. More than 50 campers, ranging in age from 7 to 49, enjoyed a week of instruction and fun with their families joining in, as well.

What began with one man's vision and 60 acres now has blossomed into a 530-acre facility that hosts more than 11,000 campers and retreat groups from across the country each year. Many of these are return groups.

"Since its inception, the FCA National Conference Center has developed a reputation for outstanding athletic and lodging facilities and an exceptional, service-oriented staff," said Joe Shell, executive director of the NCC since April 2001. "The vision for the NCC is that, 'We believe a Christ-centered experience ignites a passion for abundant living.' One trip to our facility will let you know that God has indeed blessed us with the opportunity to provide that experience."✝

There are plenty of activities to pass your time at the NCC!

'Get on the Bus'

Seventeen-year-old Carey Casey paused. He knew he wanted to go to FCA Camp. He was part of the Huddle at Andrew Lewis High School in Salem, Va., and a week of FCA Football Camp seemed like a good idea. But there were only white kids on that bus.

Not that Casey had anything against white kids, but this was 1973, and those white kids might have had something against a black kid riding their bus. Besides, the culture of the day said that he shouldn't board.

But there was that voice.

"Get on the bus, son," his father said. This was no longer an option, but instruction. Casey got on the bus.

"It wasn't popular to get on. The culture dictated that I shouldn't," Casey said. "Integration was available, and it was being promoted, but it wasn't popular."

Casey, and in reality America, is better off because he got on that bus. It propelled a life-long journey with FCA that has impacted thousands of kids of all races.

"Pop knew that if I got on the bus, it was not just going to be a blessing for his kid," Casey said. "It would be a blessing for all of America, regardless of race, because I can share my experience and the love of Christ. I have been able to tell that story countless times and help bring reconciliation to thousands of people."

After Camp, Casey came back to Salem for his senior year, where he got more involved in the FCA Huddle.

He then went on to play football at Northeast Oklahoma Junior College and the University of North Carolina, where he roomed with NFL Hall of Famer Lawrence Taylor and then Indianapolis Colts quarterbacks coach Clyde Christensen.

The older guys "mentored me as a freshman," he said. "FCA was a security for me. I could have gotten caught up in the things that tempted other guys, but I new that I would have to look into the eyes of the leaders and my friends every Thursday night. That helped me develop as a person."

After graduating from UNC, Casey attended Gordon/Conwell Seminary in Massachusetts, through the benevolence of Billy Graham, then Virginia Union School of Theology. He came on staff with FCA in 1983 as the urban director in Dallas. In order to be hired into the position, he first had to be interviewed by Dallas Cowboys coach Tom Landry, who asked the question, "If you're hired, will you be committed?"

That was a no-brainer for Casey.

In 1988, he moved to the FCA National Office in Kansas City to take the role of National Urban Director. He stayed for four years before accepting a pastoral job at Lawndale Community Church in inner-city Chicago, but returned to FCA in 1997 to head up the *One Way 2 Play—Drug Free!* program.

Now President of the FCA Foundation, Casey is continuing to serve the Lord through FCA. And it's a better organization, all because Carey Casey got on the bus. ✝

Casey has been involved in FCA since before his playing days at North Carolina.

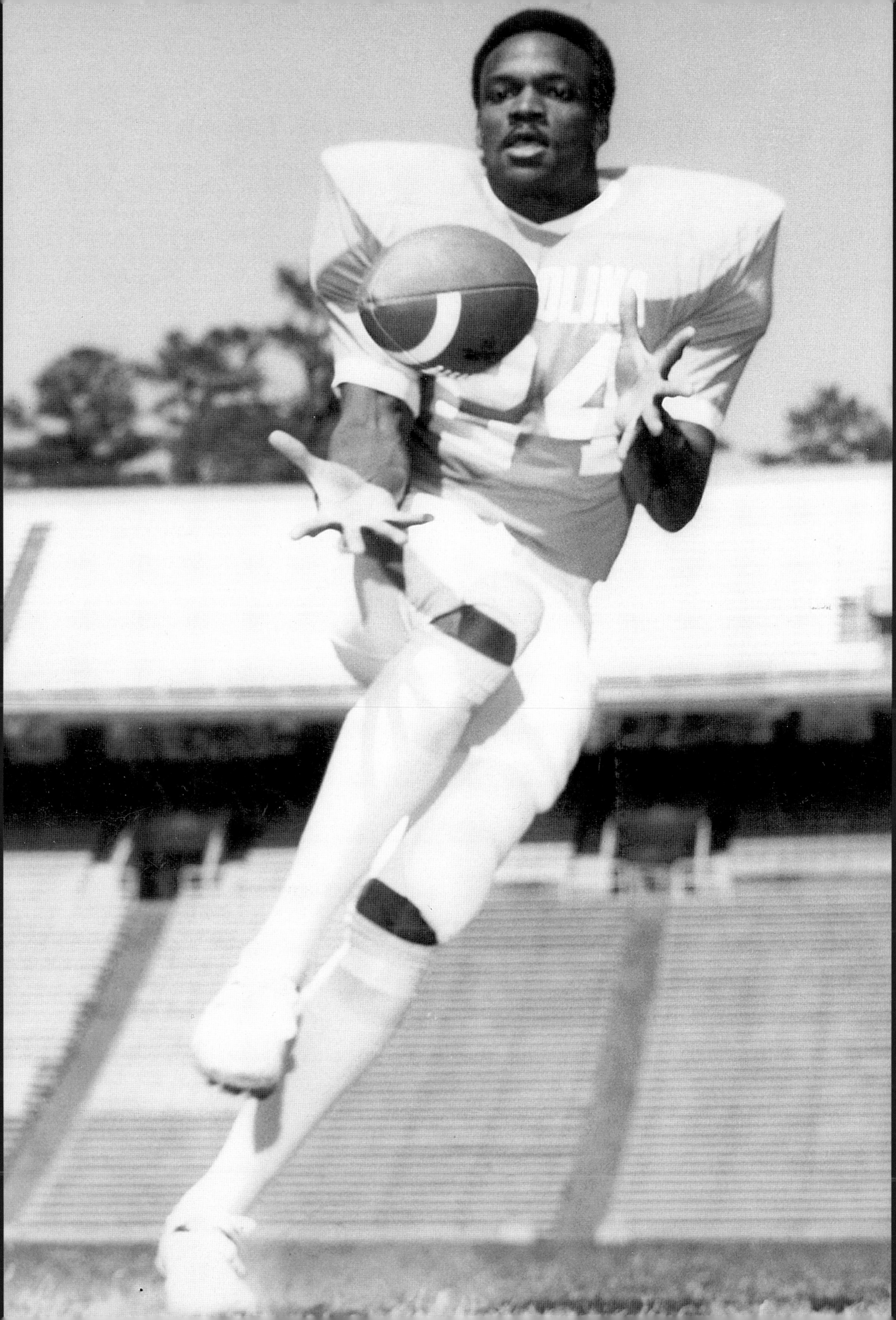

Still Focused on the Cross

The FCA logo, like the ministry it represents, has changed through the first 50 years, but it remains focused on the cross.

The first FCA logo began with discussions in 1959 about a membership pin and "covenant card" that members could obtain to show their association with FCA. Some early versions, which were not accepted as official, appeared that same year on promotional brochures, including one for the fourth annual FCA Summer Conference (predecessor to FCA Camps). Another appeared on a sheet of letterhead.

The cross was central to each logo, with athletics represented in different ways. One logo used caricatures of athletes standing at the foot of the cross ❶, while another used athletes in motion ❷. A third, which led to the official logo, used the laurel wreath ❸. (Athletes in the ancient Olympics were given laurel wreaths as a symbol of victory.)

Even in the late 1950s and early 1960s, there was sensitivity toward not favoring one sport over the others. Surely, the founding fathers of FCA realized that athletes from more sports soon would join "the movement," as it was called in the early years, making it difficult to show every sport in a usable symbol of the ministry.

At their August 1960 meeting, the FCA Board of Directors discussed the need for a unifying symbol. Chairman Roe Johnston shared his initial drawings. The October 1960 edition of *The Christian Athlete* requested suggestions from its readers.

It didn't take long to make a choice, apparently, because the official logo appeared just three months later, in the January 1961 issue of *The Christian Athlete*. The logo appeared on letterhead in September of that year.

That logo ❹ was used for the next 40 years. It included the laurel wreath, representing athletics; a banner with "FCA" in it, representing the ministry covered by His love; and beams from the ministry to the cross, representing the focus of the ministry on His sacrifice.

However, it wasn't used exclusively, which eventually led to its replacement. Some state offices added their state's shape behind the corporate logo. Some invented new ones altogether. Even the national office came up with different looks ❺.

In 2000, FCA leadership discussed the various logos used around the country and decided to investigate the idea of a new, universal logo. Research revealed more than 40 different logos in use, all representing FCA in one way or another. A year-long project, including requests for submissions, surveys of staff and volunteers, focus groups, and countless discussions led to the choice of the current logo ❻.

The current logo combines the history of a strong, influential ministry, with a progressive, active look for a ministry that is able to reach today's youth. The laurel wreath and banner still look up to the cross. The bold, wide type shows that FCA is a bold ministry, not willing to hide behind social mores that say that sharing one's faith is wrong. It also illustrates the wide reach that FCA has after 50 years of ministry.

The "action arcs" show that FCA is not willing to "rest on its laurels," instead taking the next step of reaching around the world with the message of Christ, using the influence of athletics.

Finally, even the colors chosen are symbolic. Gold represents the medal that champions receive, though we know that this treasured commodity will be "asphalt" in Heaven (Revelation 21:21). Navy is a sign of royalty and dignity. Red represents Christ's blood, shed to pay for our sins.

And, of course, the focal point of the logo is the cross. Because without the cross, FCA would have no reason to exist—or flourish—for the past 50 years, or the next 50. ✝

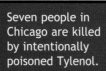

| Seven people in Chicago are killed by intentionally poisoned Tylenol. | Sixty-one year old Barney Clark becomes the first recipient of an artificial heart. | Vietnam Veterans' Memorial dedicated in Washington, D.C. | Joel Youngblood becomes first player to play for two teams (Mets and Expos) on the same day. | E.T. charms movie-going audiences. |

FELLOWSHIP OF CHRISTIAN ATHLETES

2

3

4

5

6

| The infamous "Pine Tar" game involving George Brett takes place in Yankee Stadium. | Martin Luther King, Jr.'s birthday is declared a national holiday. | North Carolina State stuns Houston to win the NCAA championship. | U.S. military invades Grenada. | Sally Ride is the first American woman in space. |

One of a Million

For every Trent Dilfer or Shaun Alexander who has lived the FCA Camp experience, there have been thousands of campers like Dennis Snow.

Snow, a sophomore in 1965 at Raytown South High School in Raytown, Mo., began participating with the FCA Huddle that was started by his football coach and Huddle leader, Vance Morris. The dozen or so young men who formed the Huddle met monthly at the home of one of its members.

In the spring of 1966, Bud Lathrop, the varsity boys basketball coach at the school, who also had some involvement with the Huddle, asked Snow if he would be interested in attending the FCA Summer Conference (Camp) at Lake Geneva, Wisc. The Raytown Kiwanis Club paid the $75 conference fee, and Snow traveled by chartered bus with 62 other area young men to Lake Geneva.

There were more than 500 attendees at the Conference, which included several high-profile university coaches and professional athletes. Activities included assemblies with dynamic speakers like Chicago Bears quarterback Bill Wade, Arkansas football coach Frank Broyles, FCA President James Jeffrey and strong-man Paul Anderson.

"I was impressed that even the celebrities participated in all of the events, including the 'Dog Patch Olympics,'" Snow said. "The one person I enjoyed meeting the most was Jerry Mays, all-pro defensive end of the Kansas City Chiefs. We were able to have a one-on-one chat for nearly two hours."

Toward the end of the week, a group photo was taken, which would later appear on the cover of the September 1966 issue of *The Christian Athlete*, the predecessor to *Sharing the VICTORY*.

A believer since the age of 6, Snow found the Conference experience to be "extremely beneficial in strengthening my faith. I felt encouraged, uplifted and challenged to live, as Jerry Mays said, 'in the image of Christ.'"

Snow had the opportunity to return to FCA Camp in 1967, this time at Green Lake, Wisc. His Conference fee was paid by a local businessman. His Huddle sent three members this time, and many of the same coaches and pro athletes returned to the Conference. When presented with an FCA Bible, Snow asked Jeffrey to inscribe his name on the "presented to" page and also asked Mays, Don Lash and Ray Hildebrand for their autographs. He still has that Bible.

Snow continues his walk of faith in his daily life as a husband and father and as a very active member and deacon of his church. He also continues a connection with FCA. He is married to Debbie Snow, editorial assistant for *Sharing the VICTORY*.

Recently, he was asked about his reflections of FCA Camp. He replied, "It was a truly great experience; very worthwhile; one of the highlights of my youth and Christian life."

Although Snow knew Jesus and had a strong relationship with Him, his life and service to the Lord were enhanced by his Camp experience. Through the generosity of others in the community, young people like Dennis Snow get to attend FCA Camp every year.

It's an investment in the future of the young person involved. And it is an investment in the Kingdom of God on Earth. ♱

Snow, who was one of the campers on the cover of The Christian Athlete following the 1966 Camp, still has the Bible he received at the 1967 Camp.

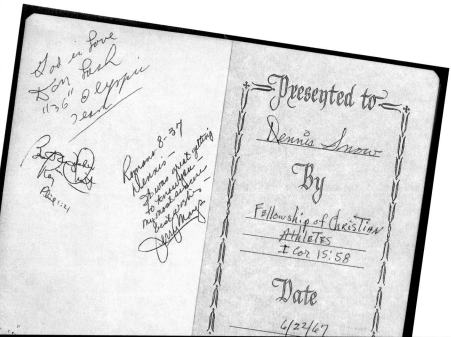

Carl Lewis wins four gold medals at 1984 Olympics in Los Angeles.

Ronald Reagan is re-elected President by a landslide.

Ghostbusters is a hit movie.

Doug Flutie's "Hail Mary" helps Boston College beat Miami in college football.

Americans spend $3 billion on spectator sports.

1985

| Lynette Woodard becomes first woman to play for the Harlem Globetrotters. | Mikhail Gorbachev becomes Premier of the Soviet Union. | Remains of the Titanic are discovered. | Coca-Cola introduces "New Coke," which promptly fails. | The number of Barbie dolls in existence surpasses the number of Americans. |

Sleek in Silver and Blue

Long before Barry Sanders made defenders miss the silver and blue Lions No. 20 jersey with his deer-like moves, even before Billy Sims made defenders wish they missed the silver and blue Lions No. 20 jersey after he ran over and through them, Lem Barney made the silver and blue Lions No. 20 jersey famous.

A smooth, yet hard-hitting cornerback out of Jackson State, Barney is second all-time in Lions history with 56 career interceptions, which ranks him 11th in NFL history. He returned seven of them for touchdowns and 1,077 return yards, both most in team history.

He was the NFL interception co-leader and defensive Rookie of the Year in 1967. He also returned kicks and was the Lions' emergency punter. He totaled 1,312 career yards on punt returns and 1,274 career yards on kickoff returns. He was named to seven Pro Bowls and was All-NFL/NFC three times.

In 1994, he was selected as one of the 75 greatest players in NFL history, commemorating the league's 75th anniversary.

Lem Barney was flat-out good.

Barney likens the walk of a Christian to the act of catching a punt or a kickoff and the attitude that is necessary to be an outstanding defensive back.

"On a kick, the ball is high in the air, forcing you to look up," Barney said. "You are tempted to keep your eyes straight ahead because the opposing team is approaching you, quickly and ferociously. But you know if you take your eyes off the football, you can fumble it and cause your team to suffer the consequences.

"Some people are better at this than others. Some seem to be able to look at both things at one time. But if you ask even the great ones, they will tell you that they focus first on 'things above' (the football) and not on the 'earthly things' (the approaching players). The Bible has instruction that fits. Colossians 3:1-2 says '...set your hearts on things above, where Christ is seated at the right hand of God. Set your minds on things above, not on earthly things.'

"Kick returners do best when they follow the coach's instructions. Teammates block according to the play called. Life is all about taking orders and being obedient to our Lord and Savior Jesus Christ. We must play by His rules and use His playbook—the Bible."

The best attribute of a good cornerback is a short memory, because he's going to get beat, and he has to be able to forget it and move on. If he's thinking about the last play, the current play likely will be worse. Barney says it's no different in life.

"We have to have short memories. If you ask God for forgiveness, He is faithful to forgive. The slate is wiped clean. Those mistakes no longer are on your record."

The football record speaks highly of Barney. After an 11-year career with the Detroit Lions, in 1992 he became the fifth cornerback selected to the Pro Football Hall of Fame.

But the Hall of Fame that Barney is most pleased with is God's. His relationship with the Lord started at an early age, when he says church was a way of life. Many years later, as a member of FCA staff, he carries a message of hope to the students and coaches of southeastern Michigan.

He always focuses on "things above" with a short memory about any failures. ✝

Barney uses the skills he learned as an NFL player in his role as FCA's area director in Detroit.

Heroes in the Faith

In a time when the sports scandal is all too familiar, positive role models have become vitally important to the ministry of FCA. Professional athletes, both men and women, who live lives of integrity are more than necessary in counteracting the negativity that is being displayed in front of the world's impressionable youth.

Professionals such as Jay Bell, Tom Lehman, Lisa Leslie, Mike Sweeney, Betsy King (see page 148), Michael Chang and Shaun Alexander have recognized the need for outspoken, Christian role models, and have chosen to become involved in FCA as a way to express their faith.

Alexander served as a Camp Huddle leader during his years as a football standout at the University of Alabama. In a 2002 *Sharing the VICTORY* article, he called his FCA Camp experience one of the "coolest" parts of his college years.

Now a Seattle Seahawk, Alexander knows the power of his platform as a professional football player.

"You never know who you are going to impact," he said. "I think it's exciting when I see kids get on my web site and say they heard me speak here or watched my game here, and say, 'I knew you were special.'" ⇨

FCA remains an athletic ministry, and athletes like 1. Lisa Leslie, 2. Jay Bell, 3. Darrell Green, 4. Tom Lehman, 5. Shawn Alexander, 6. Mike Sweeney, 7. Reggie White and 8. Jean Driscoll still have an influence.

Others, such as Larry Nelson, Dave Dravecky, Bobby Jones, Jean Driscoll, Charlie Ward, Larry Mize, David Robinson and Michelle Akers also have taken the opportunity to reach kids through the ministry of FCA.

Reggie White, the "Minister of Defense," says that FCA saved his life. "If I hadn't gone to FCA Camp when I was in high school, I probably would have wound up on the street like so many of my peers," he says.

The contribution of these pros has not gone unnoticed by the FCA family. FCA Foundation President Carey Casey says, "The professional athletes who are involved help to solidify Christ's message, not just tell FCA's story. We have many pros of many sports who are doing a tremendous job of living the Christian life on and off the field."

The list of professional athletes who have been active in the organization would be impossible to fit onto these pages. But as the ministry strives to spread the message of the Gospel to "athletes and coaches and all whom they influence," professional athletes will continue to be an integral part of the organization's success.

"I truly believe we need heroes," Casey said. "It's great when a kid can emulate not only a great catch or a great shot, but also a life of integrity."✝

6

7

USFL folds after three years.

Three-point line instituted in college basketball.

The space shuttle Challenger explodes 73 seconds after lift-off, killing its crew of seven astronauts.

Jack Nicklaus wins the Masters at age 46.

Aerobics become a popular form of exercise.

8

1987

| *The Cosby Show* is the top show on television. | John Elway engineers "The Drive" to put the Broncos in the Super Bowl. | The Dow Jones Industrial Average drops 508 points in one day; the worst stock market loss in history. | President Reagan and Mikhail Gorbachev sign arms treaty to mark the beginning of the end of the Cold War. | 18-month old Jessica McClure is rescued from a 22-foot well after 58 hours. |

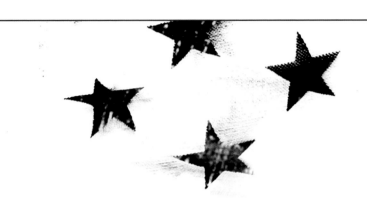

"By this all men will know
that you are my disciples,
if you love one another."

—John 13:35

Relationships

Coaches Make a Difference

There's a difference between a coach and a *Coach*.

A coach is the person in charge of practice, the one who hands out uniforms and determines who plays and how much. A *Coach* is the man or woman who breathes life into a team. His or her heart beats with that of each member of the team. A *Coach* is the person you remember—and probably still call "Coach"—20 years after your playing career is done.

† † †

Milt Cooper was a high school football coach for 24 years in Oklahoma before coming to FCA in 1998 as national director of programs. Part of his responsibility was to head FCA's coaches ministry.

"Having been in coaching for 24 years, I understand the pressures of doing so many things. It's real easy to lose your focus," Cooper said. "We have something that can help coaches stay focused and be a source of encouragement. You don't hear that very often because success is measured in wins and losses.

"It's easy to get caught in that trap, thinking 'I am successful because I won X number of games.' We forget that there is a greater call, leading the young men and women under our direction."

Though he no longer wears a whistle around his neck, Cooper is a *Coach*. He can tell you names and stats of players who played for him nearly two decades ago.

"Eric was a major college prospect at linebacker," Cooper recalled. "He had played on a state championship team for us his junior year, and we had high expectations for his senior year. Just before the eighth game of the season, he got into an argument with his little brother that ended up in a stabbing. Eric got cut across the chest and abdomen and required 120 stitches. Obviously his season was over. The major concern was for his life.

"After hearing of his injury on my way

home from our coaches meeting, I felt led to go by the house and visit with his family. When I got there, I visited with his mom and told her I came by to pray with his family. We went into Eric's bedroom with his mom, aunt, uncle and girlfriend. We circled his bed and we prayed for him.

"After we prayed I asked his mom if I could visit with Eric alone. That gave me an opportunity to share Christ with him for about the fourth time. His response was, 'I know. I know.'

"As I left, his uncle asked me if he could walk me to my car. He said, 'Coach, I want you to understand something. These are really good kids over here (on that side of town). They just don't have a daddy. Eric needs you.'

"It drove home why I was doing what I was doing. I had just been through a period where I struggled about staying in coaching. This confirmed that this was my ministry."

It's as if the event happened a week or two ago, not many years ago. Cooper acknowledges that he will be impacted forever by the players he's coached. "I have coached athletes who I may have influenced in some way, but they had a greater influence on me," he said.

He also knows that his players will carry his impact with them the rest of their lives. It's only natural. Cooper notes that a coach may spend 20 hours a week with kids during the playing season, where the average parent spends 10 minutes a week in quality one-on-one time. ⇨

1. Ron Brown, 2. Jane Albright, 3. John Wooden, 4. Grant Teaff, 5. Sylvia Hatchell, 6. Ritchie McKay, 7. Dan Reeves, 8. Ken Hatfield, 9. Steve Alford, 10. Bobby Bowden and 11. Fisher DeBerry.

I pray thee, O God,

that I may

† † †

A *Coach* wears many hats. Since so many young people are growing up in broken homes, in many cases the *Coach* is a dad or a mom to the athletes. A *Coach* can be a buddy, a counselor, a guardian, an encourager and a disciplinarian, often all at the same time.

Grant Teaff is the executive director of the American Football Coaches Association. He has served on the FCA Board of Trustees on two separate occasions, including a stint as the Chairman of the Board. He's been a highly successful football coach. But if not for the words of a *Coach*, he's not sure where he would have gone in life. He was a freshman football player at Snyder High School in Snyder, Texas, in the late 1940s. His *Coach* was Speedy Moffett.

"I had much bigger dreams than I had ability," Teaff recollects. "Coach Moffett recognized that and knew that I would struggle to get an education and become a coach, something everyone knew was my desire. He called me into his office and told me that he knew where I wanted to go, and he would tell me how to get there by giving me a secret. He told me that the secret is clearly available to everyone.

"By then, he had me entranced. What he would tell me would help a slow, small, under-talented person to achieve more than anyone thought he could. He said, 'The key is effort—every day, every way on every play, total effort.' My head was spinning because that took

a huge commitment, first of all to understand what that meant, then to have the commitment to be willing to do that."

It wasn't a kick in the pants, and it wasn't consolation. It was reaching into the life of a young man with words he could understand and embrace as his own.

"As I started to leave the room," Teaff continued, 'he said, 'There's one other thing. That means off the field as well as

on.' I can tell you, without any hesitation, that he was 100 percent right. You can't make a silk purse out of a sow's ear. What you can do is maximize every talent and ability God has given you through effort. Many times, that far exceeds what you thought you had."

† † †

Cooper and Teaff are just two of the *Coaches* who have helped FCA grow into the leader it is today. Some other well-known *Coaches* who have had the biggest impact on the ministry of FCA include Jane Albright (women's college basketball), Steve Alford (men's college basketball), Felipe Alou (pro baseball), Raymond Berry (pro football), Bobby Bowden (college football), Ron Brown (college football), Clyde Christiansen (pro football), Larry Coker (college football), Bill Curry (college football), Fisher DeBerry (college football), Joe Gibbs (pro football and NASCAR), Dick Harp (men's college basketball), Sylvia Hatchell (women's college basketball), Ken Hatfield (college football), Mark Johnson (college baseball), Jerry Kindall (college baseball), Andy Lopez (college baseball), Ritchie McKay (men's college basketball), Tom Osborne (college football), Deb Patterson (women's college basketball), Dan Reeves (pro football), Mark Richt (college football), Jim Tressel (college football), Denise Van De Walle (college volleyball), John Wooden (men's college basketball) and Kay Yow (women's college basketball).

Many of them will help carry the ministry through the beginning of the next 50 years.

They are—quite simply—*Coaches*. †

7

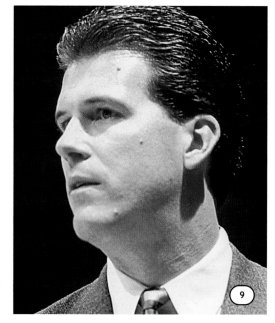

9

10

8

11

'Moore' Than a Football Coach

For 36 of his 39 years as a Texas high school football coach, G.A. Moore, Jr. has had a simple trip to work. From the Moore family farm in rural Denton County, north of Dallas, he has turned west, toward his hometown of Pilot Point, or to the east, toward the nearby town of Celina.

Moore has been one of the most successful coaches in the state's history. On November 8, 2002, he established the career record for wins by a high school football coach in the state of Texas when he won his 397th game (compared to just 74 losses and nine ties). He won eight state or division championships, one short of the state record.

But the question of direction has cropped up in many aspects of Moore's life and career. He once gave up coaching because he felt a call to the ministry. And in the midst of a winning streak that eventually would become the longest in Texas history (57 games), he took a very public stand in favor of public prayer that could have cost him his job.

Then, on the eve of the season that almost certainly would have brought him the career victories record in easy fashion as the coach at Celina, he made a decision that rocked the world of Texas football. He resigned as Celina's head coach and returned once more to Pilot Point, which had struggled in recent years.

As he was making the decision, Moore mused on the lessons of Proverbs 16:18: "Pride goes before destruction, a haughty spirit before a fall."

"People ask me, 'Why leave?'" he said. "We had a great program. Everything was in place. But things worked out in a way that there was no doubt that this was what I should do—not because I wanted it this way, but because God wanted it that way. And I want to do what He wants a whole lot more than I want to do what anybody else wants."

Moore is not about the W's and the L's, though his records would lead you to believe otherwise. He's much more interested in developing young men, through his football teams and FCA.

After his first year in coaching, he returned to his high school alma mater as head coach. One of his first moves was to begin an FCA Huddle at Pilot Point.

"Tom Landry (the late coach of the Dallas Cowboys) got me involved in 1968, at a Conference in Estes Park, Colo.," he said. "I met him and his family, and we stayed in touch. He had an Adult Chapter in Dallas, and I went to a weekend retreat with him and took some of my coaches with me. I've been involved ever since."

Moore's faith was put to the test in the fall of 2000. He took a public stand in favor of pre-game prayer at high school games. As representatives from the American Civil Liberties Union arrived to monitor the controversy, Moore retreated to the bathroom of his office, where he keeps a Bible. He flipped to the 22nd chapter of the book of Matthew, the 21st verse, "Give to Caesar what is Caesar's, and to God what is God's."

"That's when I decided that somebody needed to take a stand, and that somebody needed to be me," he said. "I prayed about it, and I told the principal that I felt like somebody needed to lead the prayer, and since I didn't want anybody getting in trouble, it should be me."

Coaches like G.A. Moore lead our young men and women onto the playing fields of high schools around the country. Fortunately, they are much more interested in what's inside the hearts of the athletes than what the bodies can do. ✝

Moore has invested his life into the lives of young people.

'I Want to Be Like Those Guys'

Gary Warner, editor of *The Christian Athlete,* couldn't have imagined the impact his photo would have. That photo, taken on a June morning in 1967 at the Blue Ridge YMCA Assembly in Black Mountain, N.C., has stood as the trademark and symbol for the Fellowship of Christian Athletes evangelical movement in spreading the Gospel of Jesus Christ for more than 35 years.

The influence represented, as a young boy with a football under his arm looks admiringly at a gathering of older boys, speaks volumes about the influence that athletes have on those around them.

The picture has served FCA's passionate story of influence remarkably well. Thousands of "No. 18" photos and plaques have hung in coaches' offices, locker rooms, athletes' rooms, business offices and homes across America, signifying the importance of role models.

Yet the story behind the photo makes you sense that God staged that moment in time for a renowned godly purpose. It was not a fluke photograph made of a kid who just happened to be standing there.

David Dean was superbly talented at age 3. He could throw a football, hit a baseball, catch extremely well, shoot a basketball and run. He had a charming demeanor. You couldn't help but notice he was special. His dad, Ray Dean, was the head football coach at Sylvan High in Atlanta. His older brother Mike was on the football team at Alabama under Coach Paul "Bear" Bryant.

Ray Dean was his school's FCA Huddle sponsor. He started bringing his family to FCA Camp on a yearly basis. At this particular Camp, he was coordinator of

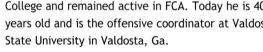

David Dean

the "Dogpatch Olympics." His son, Mike, was a Huddle leader. In fact, that was Mike's Huddle in the background of what has become known as the "influence picture" or the "No. 18 picture." As Mike went on to have a fine career at Alabama, little David developed his skills more every year.

Between his ninth and 10th grade years, David returned to Black Mountain. On a Wednesday night after the evening assembly, while sitting on the front lawn of Robert E. Lee Hall with his Huddle leader, David invited Jesus Christ into his heart. His Christian family and active church life helped him to mature spiritually.

After high school, he was awarded a football scholarship at Georgia Tech. Then, as a college football player, he returned to Black Mountain as a Huddle leader himself. By then, the "influence picture" was widely used by FCA. Even David's teammates didn't know that the kid was David. Modest David didn't tell them either.

After graduating from Georgia Tech, David started his coaching career. He spent eight years at West Georgia College and remained active in FCA. Today he is 40 years old and is the offensive coordinator at Valdosta State University in Valdosta, Ga.

More importantly, he is the Huddle sponsor of the Valdosta FCA Huddle. "I'm constantly amazed how often people bring the photo to my attention," David says. "The main question asked is, 'Do you still have the jersey?' The answer is yes."

A "Number 18" photo hangs in his office as a reminder that his players are watching him daily and that they will be influenced by the life he lives. ✝

---

*I*n Mike Dean's huddle in 1967 was a redheaded 11th grade boy named Robert Fraley from Winchester, Tenn. Robert was a superstar quarterback as a senior and signed with the Alabama Crimson Tide. He had some bright moments in big games at Alabama. Then he attended the Alabama Law School and became an attorney.

One day Fraley, who had become an agent for many head college coaches and top athletes, was introduced to PGA golfer Payne Stewart in Orlando. Stewart took a liking to

this kind and gentle man with a strong faith in God. In fact, Stewart noticed a real role model businessman in Fraley.

Several months passed and through the godly life of his new agent Fraley and a few other Christian associates, Stewart made a commitment to Jesus Christ. The man with the colorful Scottish outfits who had won the U.S. Open twice, commented, "I'm so much more at peace with myself than I've ever been in my life."

On October 25, 1999, Stewart, Fraley, his associate Van Ardan and two pilots took off on a Learjet from Orlando to Dallas in preparation for a tournament in Houston. Before their plane crashed in a field near Mina, S.D., the television networks were reporting it was missing and could not be found. Due to the loss of pressurization, the plane's autopilot kept it in the air until it ran out of fuel. Everyone aboard died from oxygen deficiency before the crash.

Several days later in the First Baptist Church of Orlando, Stewart's two-hour funeral service was televised around the world. It was a Christ-centered service that proclaimed the Gospel of Jesus Christ in a bold and clear presentation. The Golf Channel aired the service several more times. Many commented that Payne reached more people for Christ in death than he would have had he lived a long life.

His salvation and faith was highly influenced by his agent and attorney Robert Fraley, a young athlete in the "Number 18" photo. Once again, the world heard the crucial message that only through Jesus Christ can anyone gain eternal life and a home in Heaven.

Takin' It to the Streets

Six months after the tragedy of September 11, 2001, the Carlsbad (Calif.) High School FCA "put wheels under their prayers."

Led by FCA Area Director Derrick Roth and Huddle Coach Denny Cooper, a group of four adult volunteers and nine students traveled to New York to participate in the World Trade Center relief effort, and learned a lesson far more valuable than could be found in any textbook.

While in New York, the group was able to minister in many different ways. They served in two soup kitchens—one for the Ground Zero relief workers, and one for families of the victims. They witnessed to subway passengers, manned prayer stations and worked with Firefighters for Christ on Valentine's Day to distribute Valentines from around the country.

At 1 a.m. two nights before they were to leave New York, Cooper and several of the students took a cart

to Ground Zero to serve coffee and snacks to the workers.

"It was amazing," Cooper said. "We went on the trip to be of service and to help those in need. In turn, the trip blessed us every bit as much as we could have been a blessing. For each one of the kids, it was a life-changing experience."

The group used 2 Corinthians 1:3-7 as the theme for the trip:

"Praise be to the God and Father of our Lord Jesus Christ, the Father of compassion and the God of all comfort, who comforts us in all our troubles, so that we can comfort those in any trouble with the comfort we ourselves have received from God.

"For just as the sufferings of Christ flow over into our lives, so also through Christ our comfort overflows. If we are distressed, it is for your comfort and salvation; if we are comforted, it is for your ⇨

From the soup kitchens to the fire stations,
the Carlsbad Huddle got to experience the relief effort.

| Kansas defeats Oklahoma to win 50th NCAA Final Four in Kansas City. | George Bush is elected President. | 143,000,000 Americans claim affiliation with a religious group. | Faxing becomes the norm in business communication. | Ben Johnson is caught using steroids and is stripped of the 100-meter gold medal at the Olympics. |

comfort, which produces in you patient endurance of the same sufferings we suffer. And our hope for you is firm, because we know that just as you share in our sufferings, so also you share in our comfort."

✝   ✝   ✝

Sometimes, an FCA Huddle meeting can be a place of refuge. When life at school gets tough, one's friends in the Huddle can be the salve needed to restore energy.

But, as with the Carlsbad Huddle, at times the Huddle is a launching point for ministry. The young people in this Huddle found out that when they follow God's leading and "do" ministry, they are ministered to in ways they did not expect. ✝

| The Exxon Valdez oil disaster occurs. | Earthquake hits San Francisco Bay area prior to Game 3 of the World Series. | The Berlin Wall is torn down. | San Francisco's Joe Montana leads 92-yard drive in final minutes to win Super Bowl XXIII. | Gen. Colin Powell becomes the first African-American chairman of the Joint Chiefs of Staff. |

A 'Lifetime' Contract

In 1994, prior to his sophomore year at Fresno State, Trent Dilfer agreed to work an FCA Camp, but he made it clear that he was "not in it for the Christian thing, but just to coach some kids on how to play football."

The Lord, however, had a very different idea.

During the two-day preparatory period for Camp Huddle Leaders, Dilfer found himself noticing the other counselors and their actions.

"Their lifestyles as Christians weren't what I was used to," he said. "They were guys who were dedicated to Christ, but they showed it with their actions, not their words. They didn't go around praising Jesus (just) with their mouths, they did it with their lives. The first night I was there, they all sensed what was going on with me, because my heart was very hard, and I was very hard to get along with. They just broke down all the barriers with their love."

After years of merely talking the Christian life, Dilfer committed to change. And in the process, committed to helping the FCA ministry.

While at Fresno State University, he recruited kids to Camp so that they could share in the positive experience. In Tampa, Fla., as a quarterback for the NFL's Buccaneers, Dilfer also made himself well-known to FCA staff, being called by State Director Zenon Andrusyshyn, "the most involved pro athlete that we've ever seen in this area."

Dilfer continues his involvement today, primarily in his hometown of Fresno, Calif. Regional Director Joe Broussard says, "Trent is involved in three primary ways. First, he is a guide and sounding board for the FCA staff on what life is like for the high-profile, professional athlete. This has been very helpful as FCA continues to pursue relevance in the world of sports.

"Second, Trent has given his financial resources to further the Gospel through FCA Camps and the S.A.L.T. (Student-Athlete Leadership Training) program. He was a member of the original S.A.L.T. team in Fresno, and he has made sure that other college athletes have the same opportunities he had.

"The third way Trent stays involved with FCA is through speaking to churches, Camps and fundraising banquets. He is the top choice by FCA staff in California to speak whenever he is available. Trent's time away from his family is precious to him. His time is the most valuable gift he can give to FCA."✝

Dilfer and his family give much of the credit of their success to FCA.

Family Business

It's not unusual for kids to go into the "family business," especially when Mom or Dad has been in it since before they were born. So it should come as no surprise that Daniel, Quinn, Katherine and Andrew Evans are involved in FCA. Their father, Johnny Evans, has been the area director for eastern North Carolina since 1994, more than half their lives.

But that's about the only thing that is typical about the Evans children, beginning with the fact that they were born within minutes of each other 18 years ago. In the fall of 2003, the Evanses began their senior year of high school, where they all four have established themselves in the classroom, on the playing fields and in FCA leadership.

Their athletic awards are too numerous to mention, and all four are outstanding students. But what pleases Johnny and his wife, Beth, the most is how they make time to put Christ and His plan at the forefront of their lives.

"Raising quadruplets has been a challenge, though I have nothing to compare it to, since we only have the four" Johnny said. "But it's also been a great joy."

"Somewhere between the ages of 4 and 6, each one of them accepted Christ into their lives. The church we attend has a tradition. When a child comes to Christ and they are baptized, they get a chance to verbalize their testimonies. And you think, 'What can a 5-year-old say?'

"But it's unbelievable for a father to be able to sit there and listen to a 4-, 5- or 6-year-old child be able to articulate a one-minute testimony of why they put their trust in Christ."

They learned well from Johnny, who became involved in FCA in high school. A multi-sport athlete in high school who competed in football and track at North Carolina State University and then punted professionally, Johnny's life revolved around sports.

Then he met Jesus at an FCA Camp.

"It was the summer between my sophomore and junior years in high school. I felt that I had everything going well," he said. "I was already being recruited. I actually played four sports in high

The Evans family has grown up an FCA family.

school. I played two spring sports—I was a golfer and also ran track—and then played football and basketball. Things were just cruising along great, but I was confronted at that first FCA Camp that I did not have a relationship with Christ, and so I trusted Christ as my Savior when I was 16 years old.

"For me, FCA has been sort of a natural extension. It was used as an evangelistic tool to bring me to Christ; it was used as a discipleship tool to grow me in Christ and now it's being used as my calling by Christ to give back to the Kingdom."

The apples didn't fall far from the tree; all four Evans kids are leaders at the FCA Huddle at Broughton High School in Raleigh, N.C.

"They're definitely leaders by example as well as leaders on the teams that they have," said Scott Williams, the FCA area representative responsible for Broughton. "I've known them for the five years I've been on staff. I saw them in middle school, and even at that point they stood out athletically and personally. And since that time, I've seen them grow and develop not only physically, but spiritually.

"Everyone knows who the Evans kids are. One Friday morning, the boys' Huddle Coach was not able to be there. I went to see how things were going, and Daniel and Andrew were leading the Bible study."

The family business is leading people to a right relationship with Christ, using the platform and the language of sports. For Johnny and Beth Evans and their quadruplets, it's a natural fit. ✝

The Balkans are torn apart by war.

Los Angeles experiences rioting after four police officers are acquitted in the Rodney King beating trial.

Bill Clinton is elected President with only 42% of the vote.

Barney, the purple dinosaur, is a popular children's TV star.

Arthur Ashe announces he contracted A from a blood trans

A terrorist car bomb explodes at the World Trade Center, killing six and injuring hundreds.

Joe Carter hits the first come-from-behind, series-winning, walk-off home run in World Series history.

15,000 U.S. troops are sent to Somalia.

Schindler's List is a box office hit.

Michael Jordan shocks the basketball world by retiring.

Golf Royalty

Betsy King knew something was different about some of the other players on the LPGA Tour. King, a three-year veteran of the Tour, hadn't won, but she had shown potential. Yet there was a longing for the peace that some of the Christian players experienced.

She agreed to go to the 1980 Tee Off Conference, sponsored by the Christian Fellowship on the Tour. While there, she accepted Jesus Christ as her Savior and Lord.

As with any conversion to Christianity, King's life changed. Unfortunately for King, it changed for the worse. Her game deteriorated and some of her old friends told her she had lost her competitive edge when she accepted Christ. King took the "Lord" part of her conversion seriously, so she gave strong consideration to giving up the game and going into full-time ministry.

But God wanted her to use her golf skills to bring attention to her testimony. She hooked up with a new coach, who helped turn her career around. It took four years to win her first tournament, but she became a star, winning 20 tournaments between 1984 and 1989, the most of any golfer, male or female.

"I believe I'm a better golfer because of my faith," King said. "A byproduct of being a Christian is that you will be closer to your potential than you would be without the Lord.

"We need to realize that our identity is not wrapped up in what we shoot on the golf course. If we go out there and give 100 percent for 18 holes, we can walk off with our heads held high, whether we shoot a 60 or an 80."

She also notes the parallel between working with a personal coach and following God's leading.

"I have to put all my trust (regarding her swing) in my coach," she said. "I have to trust what he says, then do what he tells me. Second, I can't depend on my feelings. Finally, I always have to keep working toward the future. You can never be satisfied. It's a lifetime process.

"Similarly, we must trust God with our lives and be obedient to what He asks us to do. We cannot base our faith on feelings. And we must always push forward, realizing growth is a process."

That process brought King into lockstep with FCA Golf. She has attended FCA Golf Camps every year—many times more than one per year—for many years. She supports the Golf Ministry with her time and resources.

"No one has done more for the FCA Golf Ministry than Betsy," said John Dolaghan, then the director of the Golf Ministry, in 1996. "I've never known anyone, let alone a professional athlete, who lives their faith more than Betsy. I've never met someone with a servant attitude like hers who wants to learn more about her faith. She's as authentic as they come."

How connected was King to FCA Golf Camp? In 1989, she was tied for the lead in the U.S. Women's Open after three rounds. Right before she was ready to tee off for her final round, she called Captain Bill Lewis, the founder and then the director of the Golf Ministry, to talk about her arrival plans the next day at a Junior Golf Camp.

She won that tournament and still made her appearance at the Camp. She spent her time—two and a half days—talking more about her faith than her recent championship. FCA Camp just gives her a comfort zone.

"I like to share my testimony and speak at the buzz groups," she said. "Just being there at Camp makes a difference. I also enjoy going to Camps other than Golf, like the Athletic Camps."

Success did not change King. One of her closest friends on the tour, Barb Thomas, said, "I got to know Betsy the year before she won her first tournament. I can say that success has not changed her at all. That's a real testimony to her and her willingness to allow the Lord to work in her life."

King has continued to serve FCA as her Hall of Fame career draws to a close. She served on the FCA National Board of Trustees from 1997-2003. And she's still a regular at FCA Camps and golf events. ⇨

King really got into the swing of the FCA Golf Ministry.

World Series canceled because of Major League Baseball work stoppage.

Fifty-seven people are killed in an earthquake in Los Angeles.

Nelson Mandela is elected president of South Africa marking the end of the apartheid era.

Jordan and Israel sign peace accords.

ER debuts on television.

1994

"She's been super in terms of her participation," current FCA Golf Executive Director Dean Bouzeos said. "She takes her platform as a professional athlete seriously, and seems to take advantage of every opportunity to witness to her faith in the Lord Jesus. It has been a blessing in my life to know her and minister with her."

King is a member of the LPGA Hall of Fame. She won her 30th tournament in 1995 to qualify for the Hall,

a week after serving at another FCA Camp. She invited Dolaghan and Lewis to the induction ceremony.

"The pressure was astounding," Dolaghan said of her first victory in more than a year. "This is the most difficult Hall of Fame to get into. I think she's the best there is. She is a superstar if you put her up with anyone in any sport.

"She was in God's Hall of Fame long before she got into the LPGA Hall of Fame." ✢

Cal Ripken plays in 2,131st consecutive game.	Timothy McVeigh explodes a car bomb in Oklahoma City, destroying a federal office building, killing more than 150 people.	Bosnians, Serbs and Croats sign peace accords in the Balkans.	O.J. Simpson acquitted of double murder.	Blue M&M's debut.

1995

Professional Discipler

Dan Stavely made his living as a college football coach. He made his life serving the Lord as a discipler.

Stavely passed away in May 2003, but for the first 49 years of FCA's existence, one would be hard-pressed to find someone more intricately involved in the work of the ministry.

Stavely coached football at the University of Denver, Washington State, Stanford and Colorado. He was married to his wife, Lucille, for 66 years. He also found time to minister to and disciple college students.

"I would ask them, 'Do you believe in Christ? Do you really believe in Him? Don't just kid me. Are you willing to do something to prove it to me?' I wanted them to study specific sections of the Bible, and then we would meet to discuss what they found."

He met FCA at one of the ministry's first Camps, in Estes Park in 1958. He recognized the need for Bible study material with athletic language, so he wrote *The Game Plan*. He served on the FCA staff in Colorado until he was in his 80s, doing discipleship training. Even after he "retired," Stavely still took on new discipleship challenges.

At times, he met with students from several different campuses at the same time (Colorado, Northern Colorado and Colorado State), having up to four meetings per week with each student.

The meetings all revolved around the same thing: "If you study the Bible, you get the message and an assurance that if you make mistakes, which we all do, you can go to the Lord, ask His forgiveness, recommit yourself to doing those things and He will bless you."

He was inducted into the Colorado Sports Hall of Fame in 1988 and the inaugural class of the FCA Hall of Champions in 1991.

And then, in May 2003, his final induction was to God's Hall of Fame, the best of all. ✝

Stavely spent his life as a coach—of young football players and young Christians.

One 'Happy Camper'

The first thing Tony Dungy did when he became a head coach in the NFL might surprise you. He didn't buy a new, fancy car. He didn't change his wardrobe to reflect his new salary. He found out the dates of the FCA Coaches Camp in Black Mountain, N.C., so he could bring his new staff to the event.

Dungy was named head coach of the Tampa Bay Buccaneers on January 22, 1996. That summer, Dungy and his staff made the 10-hour drive from Tampa to the hills of western North Carolina. It was a tradition that he maintained in each of his six seasons as the Bucs' head coach.

"I don't think I'd be fired for messing up coaching, but I certainly could lose my job over screwing up the summer trip," said Clyde Christensen, Dungy's offensive coordinator at Tampa Bay.

"It's a great family experience, and there are very few of those available to a coach. Your kids are being ministered to and they're meeting good kids. Your wife is having a blast, because she's with other coaches' wives. The atmosphere is extremely low-key."

That's a good way to describe Dungy. "He doesn't rant and rave around the sideline," Christensen said. "He's going to be classy. He's going to treat people with respect. And he's going to be humble and gracious."

Dungy has plenty of reasons to brag, if he wanted to. In the 10 years prior to his arrival in Tampa Bay, the Buccaneers had nine seasons in which they lost at least 10 games and were 43-111 overall. In his six seasons, he compiled a 54-42 regular-season record and had four playoff appearances, including reaching the 1999 NFC Championship Game.

In his first season with the Colts, he led the team to a 10-6 record and a berth in the AFC playoffs. A defensive specialist, Dungy's first team in Tampa went from 27th in the league in total defense to 11th. The next five years, the worst team ranking was ninth.

Dungy was a three-year NFL cornerback with the Pittsburgh Steelers and San Francisco 49ers. He played quarterback (and guard for the basketball team) for the University of Minnesota, where he won the Big Ten Conference's Scholar Athlete Medal after his senior year.

You'd never know those accolades belonged to Dungy if you waited for him to tell you. When he's at Camp, he's just as likely to be picking the brain of a high school coach as he is to be giving out advice. He's as comfortable in the back of the food line as he is at the head table.

"You get to talk to coaches and know that what you're going through isn't all that different from what everybody else is going through," he said about why he enjoys the Camp experience. "You get to share some things and encourage some other people, and draw encouragement from them." ✛

Dungy (right in photo at left) feels as much at home at an FCA Camp as he does on an NFL sideline.

| Centennial Olympic Games in Atlanta. | The Taliban seizes control in Afghanistan. | "Mad cow" disease forces the destruction of more than 1 million cattle in Britain. | "Tickle Me Elmo" dolls are the rage. | Michael Jordan comes back from two-year hiatus to lead the Chicago Bulls back to the top of the NBA. |

1996

| Scottish scientists announce the first cloning of a mammal. | Princess Diana of Wales is killed in a car crash in Paris. | The U.S sends aircraft carriers to the Persian Gulf with a warning to Iraq that it must allow U.N. weapons inspectors to do their work. | Tiger Woods wins the Masters by 12 strokes, the largest margin ever. | The *Sojourner* spacecraft sends spectacular images from the surface of Mars. |

A Winner in Every Way

Nick Hyder had few equals. As the head coach at Valdosta High School from 1974-96, he earned seven Georgia state football championships and three *USA Today* national championships. His 28-year coaching record was 302-48-5. But those are just stats.

As with many coaches on the high school level who pour their whole lives into the lives of their students, Hyder was a hero far beyond the football field.

"Nick cared as much for the non-athletes as he did for his football players," said Doug Scott, FCA's area director for South Georgia. "They knew he cared for them because he demonstrated it in his actions."

Hyder took over a program that had been led by another coaching legend, Wright Bazemore. Under Bazemore, Valdosta had won 268 games, 15 state championships and three national championships. The winning tradition dated all the way back to 1913.

Hyder's first team went 3-7, but he won 10 games the next season and nearly 200 in the next 17 years. He died of a heart attack in 1996, but his presence still is being felt in the town of slightly more than 50,000 near the Georgia-Florida border.

"Nick never would cut a player," Scott said. "They had as many as 115 or 120 players dress out. He would keep any player on the squad who could hold up a jersey. John Federico, a physically handicapped player, was allowed to suit up. In the state championship game one year, he got to play a down to a standing ovation. Federico says that event changed his life.

"Everywhere you go in Valdosta, Nick's spirit is still alive in the hearts of people," Scott said. "It's unbelievable how much people still talk about him and what he stood for."

It had to be more than what he did on the football field—and it was.

Hyder cared more about his players' spiritual health than he did their physical attributes. He started every practice with a voluntary prayer, though nearly everyone participated. He chose a Scripture verse to serve as a theme for each day's practice as well.

"He used to say, 'I don't live to coach, but to lead kids to Jesus Christ. Through doing this, it has made me a better coach,'" Scott said.

On game day, the coaches and players would gather on the sideline and say the Lord's Prayer. After games with their cross-town rival, Lowndes High, the two teams would gather at the 50-yard-line for a post-game prayer.

"Even though that was one of the biggest rivalries in high school football in the country, the coaches at Lowndes loved Nick," Scott said.

Hyder just wasn't afraid to share and show his faith.

"Nick was a rare breed," FCA President Dal Shealy said. "Being the outstanding and successful coach that he was, he was invited to speak at football clinics all across the nation. When he shared his philosophy about how he used Scripture verses as themes for each day, he was asked how he could do that at a public school. His response was very simple. 'I'm the head coach!'"

Hyder always led his team in prayer in the locker room before they took the field. He used to say, "If they ever tell me I can't pray with my team, I will get out of coaching."

His teams always sang the song "Amen" before they left the locker room. "That resonated through that place," Scott said.

Hyder acknowledged that his success helped raise his platform. He also noted that FCA helped bridge that gap. "FCA has been God's bridge during the 60s, 70s, 80s and 90s, particularly in our public and private schools," he said in a 1991 article in FCA's magazine *Sharing the VICTORY*.

"It's not just one segment of athletes, not just the players or not just the athletes. It's through coaches and athletes and all whom they influence, and that includes everybody. We do not exclude anyone, and I like that about FCA."

Hyder was Valdosta's Huddle Coach for most of his 22 years. In the absence of a staff person in the area for part of that time, he served as the pseudo-staff ⇨ person. He sent out a regular newsletter to other

Mark McGuire hits 70 home runs; shattering the old record.

Violence escalates in Kosovo.

Frank Sinatra dies at 82.

President Bill Clinton is impeached.

Sen. John Glenn, 77, returns to space aboard the shuttle Discovery.

coaches in the area, publicizing FCA and sharing the Good News of Jesus Christ.

In that newsletter, he shared his top five priorities in life: God, family, country, academics (vocation) and friends. His nationally ranked Wildcats came in a distant sixth.

After his death, FCA dedicated the Nick Hyder Memorial Prayer Garden at the Black Mountain (N.C.) Camp. He also was inducted into the FCA Hall of

Champions—the only high school coach so honored—in 1994.

"Nick and I were college teammates," Shealy said. "When I went back to Carson-Newman as head football coach, I tried to hire him on two different occasions. He said no both times. He told me, 'I am called to be a high school football coach. If through FCA, I can get them to understand about Jesus Christ, then I have been a successful coach.'" ✟

Hyder was an intenese competitor, but his joy came from leading young people to Christ.

| At Columbine High School in Colorado, two students kill 12 other students and a teacher before turning their guns on themselves. | Bill Clinton is acquitted in his impeachment trial. | World population reaches 6 billion. | College student Shawn Fanning invents the Napster program for Internet music shopping. | John F. Kennedy, Jr. and his wife and sister-in-law die when their small plane crashes into the ocean. |

Football Pastor

The first thing you notice about Ken Smith is his sense of humor. That's partly because as you approach him, the people around him already are laughing, most likely at something he just said.

It doesn't take long, however, to realize the depth of character behind the humorous exterior. Ken Smith cares about the people around him. He has served three major universities as chaplain, having served at Florida State for 10 years and South Carolina for five before coming to Mississippi State.

When Mississippi State running back Keffer McGee drowned during the preseason in 1997, Bulldogs coach Jackie Sherrill called South Carolina coach

Brad Scott and said, "Don't you have a chaplain?" When Scott said he did, Sherrill said, "I need him."

As the director of player development for the Bulldogs, Smith supervised all areas of what the players did off the field. A big part of that revolved around FCA.

"As a pastor (for more than 20 years), I could do all the youth programs at church I wanted to, and some kids (still) were not going to come to my church," he said. "But the FCA could do something and we'd get kids involved. That's why I'm a strong believer in FCA as a pastor and as a (former) Board member." ⇨

Sony's PlayStation 2 launches in the U.S. and is sold out by early morning the first day.

142 climbers make it to the summit of Mt. Everest—the most ever in a single year.

Reality TV mania hits the U.S. with *Who Wants to Be a Millionaire* and *Survivor*.

George W. Bush becomes President in a close and contentious election.

Y2K scare amounts to nothing as the new millennium arrives with few glitches.

2000

Smith's introduction to FCA occurred in 1969 when he was a high school football coach in Leesburg, Fla. "I was in a 'Remember the Titans' situation," he said. "I was the defensive coordinator at Leesburg High School, which was under court order to integrate.

"One of the coaches, a black man named Hubert Dabney, was a strong Christian. We were looking for a way to get all the kids on the same page, so we started a Bible study. That was my first contact with FCA.

"I always saw FCA as a way for the church to be in the marketplace. Where churches couldn't go, FCA could go. Every church I've ever pastored, we had FCA in our budget. I want pastors to know that."

He served on the FCA Board of Trustees from 1995-2001. He speaks to an average of 90 Huddles per year from Maryland to Texas and is a regular featured speaker at FCA Camps. ✞

Smith served Jackie Sherrill (left, above) as director of player development.

| 2001 | Foot-and-mouth disease in Europe's cattle herds causes widespread panic and economic devastation. | Expansion Arizona Diamondbacks win the World Series against the New York Yankees. | Islamic terrorists hijack airplanes and crash them into the World Trade Center in New York and into the Pentagon in Washington, D.C. More than 3,000 lives are lost. | Anthrax-poisoned letters kill a Florida man and cause the shut down of post offices in Washington, D.C. | The United States invades Afghanistan and liberates it from the Taliban. |

Finding Ministry in All the Right Places

Crystal Traugott was doing what she normally does when she heard the news. She was ministering—this time at an FCA Leadership Camp at St. Simons, Ga. But this Camp would result in a ministry opportunity that was far from what Crystal was accustomed.

It began when a fellow Huddle leader instructed her to go to the Camp office and call home immediately.

"I didn't know why until I made the call, but I knew it was something serious," Crystal said. "My dad and two younger brothers had been in an accident. My 13-year-old brother Daniel had been airlifted and was in serious condition."

When she went back into the evening session, the whole group was praying for Daniel. Unfortunately, Crystal's 15-year-old sister Cheryl, who had not yet heard the news, was one of the students in the group when the announcement was made.

"My sister came back to me crying," Crystal said. "A lot of Huddle leaders came back and prayed with us.

Then everyone started worshipping. I had just prayed that God would fill that place with His presence."

Crystal and Cheryl were driven home to Orlando and were taken straight to the hospital. By the time they arrived, however, Daniel had been pronounced dead. Doctors later revealed that he likely had died on impact.

Daniel Traugott hadn't been a typical teenage boy. He knew his Savior intimately, and he was passionate about sharing Him with others. Playing the guitar and writing worship songs by age 11, Daniel had wanted to be a missionary. "God has been faithful to use Daniel's life to share the Gospel with more people than Daniel ever could have imagined," Crystal said.

"That afternoon I had shared with the girls in my Huddle how they needed to be ready to share Christ at any time," she continued. "God really prepared me that day." ✝

Crystal's family (right) is important to her. So when the news of her brothers' and father's accident reached the Camp, her "extended" family was able to minister to her, including breaking into spontaneous worship (top left).

Now That You Mention It...

Danny Lotz was a 28-year-old Air Force dentist in the summer of 1965. His base commander allowed him to take time off each summer to attend FCA Camps (then called Conferences).

Anne Graham was a high school junior in Asheville, N.C., who attended an FCA Camp at nearby Black Mountain. She was a shy girl who was somewhat reluctant to share that her parents were Billy and Ruth Graham.

Anne walked into the room for the evening session and caught Danny's eye. "When you're 28 years old and single, everybody is trying to fix you up," Danny says, "but they weren't looking at the 17-year-olds."

Danny introduced himself to Anne and they hit it off. Though he didn't share it with her, Danny was convinced right away that he had found the woman of his dreams.

After visiting with her parents until midnight, he went back to his room and called his mother in Northport, N.Y. He woke her up and told her that he had met the woman he was going to marry. The conversation went something like this:

Danny: Mom, quit praying. I've found my future wife.

Mom: You're kidding.

Danny: No, Mom, I'm serious. I just know she's the one for me.

Mom: Well, son, she'd better be Billy Graham's daughter!

† † †

Danny and Anne married in 1966. Danny is a retired dentist in Raleigh, N.C. and Anne is one of the best-known evangelists in America. Their love for FCA runs deep and long. He has served on the Board of Trustees for most of the past 25 years, and their generosity toward the ministry is legendary.

Their whole family is involved in the ministry. Jonathan, the oldest, is on staff with FCA in the Fresno, Calif., area. Morrow, their second child, lives in Raleigh, N.C. She and her husband, Traynor Reitmeier, run the Huddle at Broughton High School, where Johnny Evans' four kids are Huddle leaders (see page 146).

Rachel Ruth, the youngest is married to Steven Wright, who used to be on staff with FCA in the Raleigh area. He now serves as a coach and teacher, and she's a stay-at-home mom.

FCA Camps still are integral in their lives. Danny has been to FCA Camp every year since 1964 and Anne has missed only a few.

"Our kids grew up going to FCA Camp," Danny says. "You think of important things in your life. I met my wife through FCA. I am practicing in Raleigh because of an FCA guy, so I met my vocation through FCA. And FCA has done more for my children than anything else in their lives. Both of our daughters met their spouses through FCA.

"FCA has been my life." ✛

Danny and Anne in the mid 1980s (with their kids) and today.

| Scandal and corruption result in the bankruptcy of Enron, World Com and other American corporations. | Halle Berry becomes the first African-American woman to win an Academy Award. | Nine miners are rescued in Pennsylvania after 77 hours trapped in a flooded coal mine. | Snipers prey on D.C. suburbs. | Queen Elizabeth II celebrates 50 years on the British throne. |

2003

The San Antonio Spurs knock off three-time defending champion Los Angeles Lakers en route to NBA title.

The space shuttle Columbia explodes upon re-entry into Earth's atmosphere, killing its crew of seven.

SARS ("severe acute respiratory syndrome") infects hundreds in Asia and Canada causing worldwide concern.

Lance Armstrong wins his record-tying fifth straight Tour de France.

The United States invades Iraq and ousts dictator Saddam Hussein.

"'I know the plans I have for you,'
declares the Lord, 'plans to pros-
per you and not to harm you, plans
to give you hope and a future.'"

—Jeremiah 29:11

FUTURE

Future

Sports

During the early years of FCA, baseball and football were the dominant sports in American society. In the 1960s and 70s, basketball joined the "big two" as primary sports. As FCA enters its second half-century, the ministry recognizes that not all athletes play the traditional sports, instead participating in surfing, wakeboarding and other water sports, to mountain climbing, skateboarding and other extreme sports, to lacrosse, field hockey and other team sports. FCA now has Camps in 22 different sports. ⇨

School-based

There are 28 million young people between the ages of 12 and 18 who participate in competitive athletics in the U.S. Less than 7 million of those participate in school-based sports, meaning there is a vast pool of young athletes who will not be reached with the traditional school-based FCA model. FCA is delving into the club-based sports scene with team Bible studies and curriculum for individual athletes. ⇨

Gender

More than 50 percent of the participants in FCA Leadership Camps—the training ground for future FCA leaders—are female. Sports no longer is a male-dominated field. Professional leagues are popping up for female athletes and the professional tours of golf and tennis are gaining popularity, rivaling that of their counterparts for men. FCA recognizes that in order to reach the populace with the influence of athletes and coaches, women must be included. ⇨

Race

African-Americans no longer are the largest minority in America. Hispanic-Americans outnumber African-Americans and within 20 years may outnumber Caucasians. Race relations no longer means allowing Blacks and Whites to get along on the playing field. It means blending the many cultures that now make up mainstream America. FCA is in nearly every state and has a goal of reaching every campus with the Good News of Jesus Christ. Red and Yellow, Black and White, they are precious in His sight—and the sight of FCA. ⇨

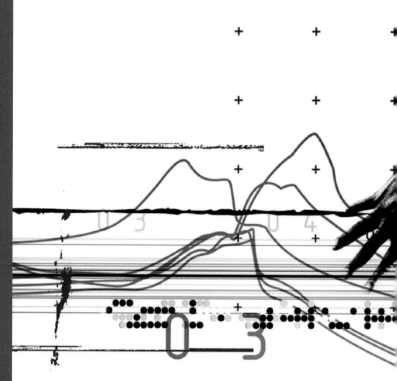

Technology

Cell phones, pagers, PDAs, computers, the Internet, game systems for the television and computer, MTV, videos and DVDs—the list of distractions is endless. While all of these things can keep young people—including student-athletes—from refining their skills, they also can serve as obstacles in building a relationship with the Creator of all things—Jesus Christ. FCA uses and will continue to use the technology avail able to reach athletes and coaches and all whom they influence with the saving grace of God. ⇨

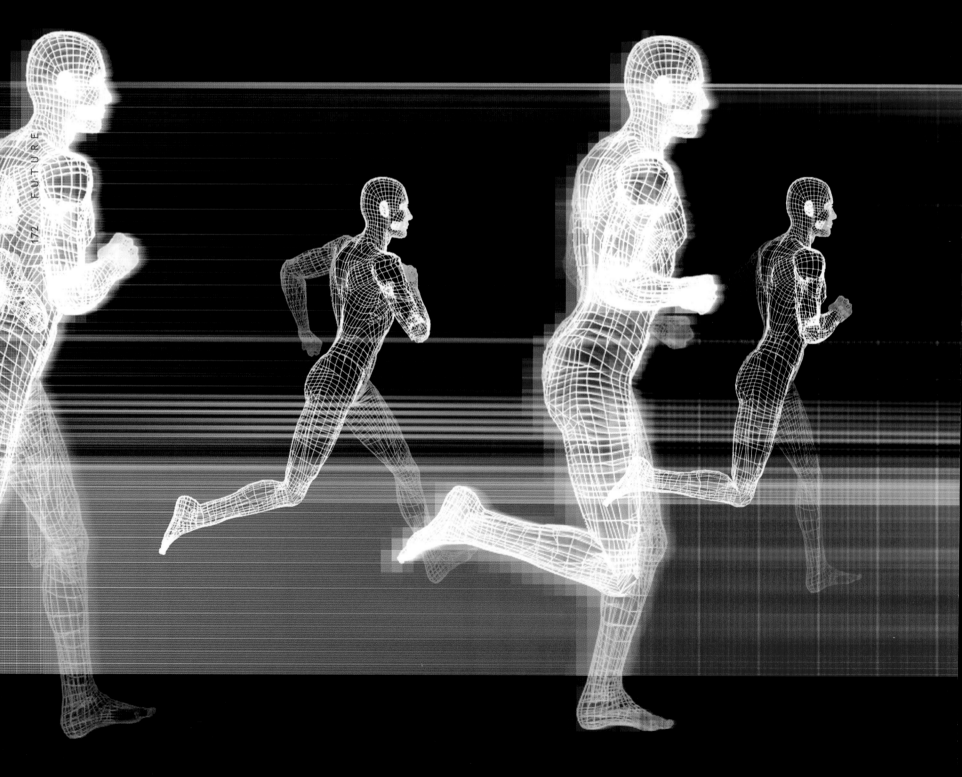

Ministry

There are many hurdles and obstacles standing in the way of FCA "seeing the world impacted for Jesus Christ through the influence of athletes and coaches." As it enters its second 50 years, FCA will continue to focus on the cross, where Christ paid the ultimate price for the sins of the world. Nothing will get in the way of that message. ✟